Praise for *Flourish*

I'm amazed at all the practical information Mary Jo Tate has included in this book. As homeschool moms, we're trying to juggle at least thirteen balls at a time. If you want to flourish and find balance in your life, you've come to the right place. I wish I'd had this book when my kids were born, because it would have made my life a lot easier.

KERRY BECK

HowToHomeschoolMyChild.com

This is it—the one complete life management 101 course you need! Mary Jo has put the essential information you need to run your home, run a business, homeschool your kids, and build a Christian heritage in your family all in one easy place. If you're a mom with kids at home, you'll find wisdom here that will lead you into joy.

DEBRA BELL

Author of *The Ultimate Guide to Homeschooling*

Mary Jo Tate addresses the very concerns and fears I hear over and over again from moms. This book is really sixteen in one, covering every topic from using your time wisely and training your children in responsibility and service to homemaking and running a home business. She transparently shares her unique challenges as a single parent, not only encouraging other solo parents, but also equipping married moms with practical tips to help the single-parent family.

VICKI BENTLEY

Author of *The Everyday Family Chore System* and *Home Education 101*

I have learned a shocking truth: Achieving balance in my life is not a myth! *Flourish* is a fabulous book that every homeschool mom needs to read! Mary Jo Tate gives hope and help to frazzled mothers so they can achieve balance and find margin in their lives. Each chapter includes activities and step-by-step exercises to put these plans into action in your own life. This book is a keeper, and it will stay next to me for a long time!
LEE BINZ
www.TheHomeScholar.com

Mary Jo brings the keen insight and outlook of a new millennium to the ideas and ideals I began homeschooling with thirty years ago. I want to homeschool again with Mary Jo's book beside me, but my three adult children are probably too busy . . .
JAN BLOOM
BooksBloom.com

If you need assistance with *anything* related to sanity, motherhood, organization, sanity, child-rearing, stress relief, and sanity, Mary Jo Tate has been there and done that. This book is destined to become the go-to reference on just about every aspect of motherhood.
JOANNE CALDERWOOD
Author of *The Self-Propelled Advantage*

Mary Jo Tate's *Flourish* is a comprehensive and creative corrective to a homeschool community that has lost sight of one our basic values—quality of life. It is an intensely practical and wise book. If you are homeschooling or intend to, read it.
MICHAEL CARD
Award-winning author and singer-songwriter

Homeschooling has a lot of moving parts. And if you add in a home business, daily living can seem overwhelming. When Mary Jo Tate found herself unexpectedly single with four sons to support, she buckled down and learned how to structure her life, homeschool, and home business in a way that allowed her family to grow together. *Flourish* shares Mary Jo's life-tested strategies and provides encouragement and organization tools that really work.
JANICE CAMPBELL
Everyday-Education.com

Flourish is filled to the brim with inspirational stories of a seasoned mother who has lived a life of faith and integrity and who shares from wisdom invested in the trenches of homeschooling. My friend Mary Jo clearly defines exceedingly practical ideas for goal setting, life management, and making the homeschooling life work for you.
SALLY CLARKSON
Author of *Seasons of the Heart* and coauthor of *Educating the WholeHearted Child*

If you desire to balance the time God has given you to accomplish all that He has asked of you, *Flourish* is the book that will help you do it! This book has encouraged me—as a homeschool mom and small business owner, widowed and now remarried—to take action. Mary Jo's advice is invaluable for anyone who desires to find balance in their lives.
CATHY DIEZ-LUCKIE
Figures in Motion

Balancing the demands of raising a family, educating children at home, ministering to one's community, and working to add to the household income is both a sharply-honed science and a well-appointed art. Mary Jo Tate demonstrates beautifully how to flourish in a life with such pressing demands, and she does it with grace and the wisdom that comes with experience. *Flourish* is the book I've been waiting to read for nearly two decades of homeschooling my own children.

KENDRA FLETCHER
Author of *Preschoolers and Peace*

Flourish is a life coach/handbook for every homeschool mom. Whether your life needs a minor tweak or a major overhaul, Mary Jo Tate has no-nonsense advice for everything from managing your to-do list and homeschooling your children to starting a small business. Even if you implement only a few of her suggestions, *Flourish* could change your life, clarify your direction, and help you find productivity and peace. A must-read for everyone who struggles with getting it done.

JEANNIE FULBRIGHT
Award-winning author of Apologia's Young Explorer Series

Struggling with balance in your life? Look no further. This guide offers real help and solutions that work. I'm too busy to waste my time on fluff, and Mary Jo Tate completely understands the busy mom's need for answers *now*! With a touch of humor, real-life illustrations, and even help for moms who work at home, this book has become my go-to resource.

FELICE GERWITZ
Founder of the Ultimate Homeschool Radio Network

I'm a time-management failure. My work-at-home-mom years bordered on chaos. Mary Jo Tate calmly and kindly has opened my eyes with these wise words: "Find peace in the space between the ideal and reality." Finally, I have hope for an ordered life!
Maggie Hogan
Creative Director, Bright Ideas Press

We homeschool moms wear many hats—wife, mom, teacher, principal, chauffeur, homemaker, chef, housekeeper, decorator, supervisor, child trainer, etc. And the list doesn't always stop there. Some of us are also contributing to the family's income by working from home or holding down outside jobs. There are days when it all feels overwhelming, especially when some of those hats get caught in a gusty whirlwind and blow off. Mary Jo Tate understands this and has learned the fine art of balance. Within these pages, she graciously shares the wisdom she has learned along her journey and generously provides the practical steps needed so that you too can find balance. Are you ready to flourish?
Terri Johnson
Knowledge Quest

Spending time in these pages is like chatting with a wise friend over coffee. Born from the author's experiences as a busy homeschooling mom who also works from home, *Flourish* has made me excited about initiating some changes and doing things differently. Mary Jo inspires her readers to action with solutions that are both practical and flexible. I love how her honesty, transparency, and encouragement invite us to take baby steps toward living a more balanced, fulfilled life. Moms in every circumstance will find hope and help not simply to exist, but to flourish.
Kim Kautzer
WriteShop.com

Life-changing! That's how you'll feel about *Flourish*. Not only does Mary Jo Tate share the unique journey of becoming the sole financial support for her family, but she also shares practical and creative ways to thrive while overcoming the many obstacles common to homeschool moms. If you've ever longed for an older godly woman to encourage you in the areas of mothering, homeschooling, and home business—one who has really been there—you'll love the wisdom found in this book!

Jill Novak
Author of *Every Day Is a Gift: Journal the Ordinary Moments of Your Extraordinary Life.*

Not only does Mary Jo Tate address how we can evaluate and organize our priorities, but she also offers sound words of encouragement in training up our children to take on responsibility, share the load in managing the home, and incorporate education in all aspects of life. Even with our fourth and last child graduating this year, there is still much I will be taking with me from this book! I know that *Flourish* will be a blessing and an answer to prayer for many struggling moms out there trying to keep their heads above water.

Amy Pak
Home School in the Woods

This book is a mentor's manual for navigating the homeschool years. You can go to it over and over again for wisdom and answers to what you're facing. Invaluable.

Elizabeth Smith
Former Director of Development, Home School Foundation
Wife of Mike Smith, president of HSLDA

This book is a breath of fresh air! Every page is filled with transparency, encouragement, and wisdom. Mary Jo gathers real-life wisdom from years of experience and shares it in a concise, easy-to-understand manual for every mother trying to establish healthy family and business habits.

SHIRLEY SOLIS
Family Catalyst at BuildingCharacterwithChildren.com

I have to confess that some days we're just surviving at our house. It's tough to juggle homeschooling, family life, and a home business. And I know I'm not the only homeschool mom out there struggling. We all could use some encouragement every now and then. Filled with practical ideas, *Flourish* will help you to finally put down the burdens God never intended you to carry. Mary Jo will help you move beyond survival and actually flourish in the roles God has given you. A must-have for every homeschool mama's nightstand!

GENA SUAREZ
Publisher, *The Old Schoolhouse* Magazine

The chapter on home business is packed with practical advice. It made this CPA smile! Warm, readable, and so doable. Mary Jo Tate is a business consultant who acts like a friend sharing a cup of tea and giving you advice with every sip!

CAROL TOPP, CPA
MicroBusinessForTeens.com

With humor and grace, Mary Jo Tate shows you how to lighten your burden and accomplish what's really important. This is real, practical help and solid encouragement with no guilt!

HAL & MELANIE YOUNG
Authors of *Raising Real Men*

Flourish

BALANCE FOR HOMESCHOOL MOMS

Flourish
BALANCE FOR HOMESCHOOL MOMS

MARY JO TATE

Flourish:
Balance for Homeschool Moms

Published by
Apologia Educational Ministries, Inc.
1106 Meridian Plaza, Suite 220/340
Anderson, Indiana 46016
www.apologia.com

Lyrics from "The Poem of Your Life"
used by permission of Michael Card.

Manufactured in the USA
First Printing: April 2014

ISBN: 978-1-940110-36-3

Printed by Bang Printing, Brainerd, MN

Cover Design: Doug Powell
Book Design: Andrea Kiser Martin

Unless otherwise indicated, Scripture quotations are from:
New American Standard Bible® (NASB) © 1960, 1977, 1995
by the Lockman Foundation. Used by permission.

Other Scripture quotations are from:
The Holy Bible, New International Version (NIV) © 1973, 1984
by International Bible Society, used by permission of
Zondervan Publishing House.

English Standard Version (ESV) © 2001 by Crossway Bibles,
a division of Good News Publishers.

The Holy Bible, New King James Version (NKJV)
© 1982 by Thomas Nelson, Inc.

For my parents,
Jim and Rosemary Alinder

Contents

"Edit" Your Stuff
Meals
Take Action!

Why Should You Homeschool?
How Should You Homeschool?
When Should You Homeschool?
Where Should You Homeschool?
Get Real with Realistic Expectations
A Day in Our Life
Nurture a Love of Reading
Teach Children of Different Ages Together
Encourage Independent Learning
Delegate
Technological Tutors
Systematize for Success
More Than Academics
Take Action!

Rest in God's Faithfulness
You're Still a Family
Foster a Strong Sense of Family Identity and Unity
Don't Be a Lone Ranger
Make Homeschooling Work
Balance Work and Family
Take Care of Yourself
How You Can Help a Single-Parent Family
Be Sensitive to Their Concerns and Needs
Offer Encouragement, Prayer, and Counsel
Offer Material Help
Offer Your Time

Take the Initiative
Take Action!

Foreword
by Tina Farewell

For eighteen years, my husband, five children, and I spent about six months each year traveling across America and ministering to home educators through speaking, operating Lifetime Books and Gifts, and publishing our *Always Incomplete Resource Guide*. We retired from Lifetime in 2005 but continue to work with homeschoolers through speaking and writing.

As I've talked with thousands of homeschool moms over the years, I've come across the same struggles again and again. Many moms are overwhelmed. They have high ideals and feel guilty for not always living up to them. They are so busy that they risk burning out. Mary Jo Tate addresses these challenges, and many more, in this book. She offers much-needed solutions to help moms flourish.

I have known Mary Jo for over ten years, have spent time with her family in her home, and have seen her flourishing in many situations. She is a mature, experienced mother and veteran homeschooler of four sons, two of whom have graduated. She has developed and practiced what she teaches through many years of challenges. Mary Jo can be trusted. She tells her story not to be put on a pedestal, but because she daily experiences God's grace and freedom through the power of the Holy Spirit. This story of His faithfulness needs to be shared.

As I write this foreword, Mary Jo is getting out of her comfort zone in Mammoth Cave. Does she like caves? No. Does she want to be inside that deep, dark place? You've got to be kidding! So what compelled her to be there? Her thirteen-year-old son, Thomas. He simply dreamed of having an adventure by encountering a fascinating part of God's creation—so Mary Jo set aside her fear in order to make a memory with Thomas. That's the kind of woman she is—a woman who walks through life honestly sharing her fears, joys, sorrows, challenges, and triumphs.

Mary Jo shares practical, real-life principles to give your family life balance and to help make your personal and business lives successful. Being a single mom for the last thirteen years gives her a special understanding and empathy for others in challenging situations. Her approach is flexible, and she wisely urges readers to adapt her strategies to their unique circumstances and to the various seasons of life. If you have many young children, your days will be very different from those of a mom of two teens. If you are caring for an elderly parent, field trips and extracurricular activities may need to be put on hold for a time.

Whatever your situation, it is difficult to accomplish much without managing your life wisely. This book helps you evaluate how you are using your time, set and follow appropriate goals, and deal with the inevitable interruptions. As Mary Jo points out, opportunity does not equal obligation. Saying no to some things allows you to say yes to more important things.

Much of Mary Jo's teaching can be summarized in her counsel to "find peace in the space between the ideal and reality." Each time I pondered that phrase in the manuscript, I found more rest and peace. Having the right attitude, undergirded by the love of Christ, squelches guilt, fear, perfectionism, resentment, whining, and martyrdom.

Caring for ourselves helps our bodies, minds, and spirits become sharper and better able to meet life head on. Having a community of like-minded, supportive people is vital. Years ago Richard Swenson, author of *Margin* and *The Overload Syndrome*, stated, "The more radical you become, the more support you need." The fellowship of a community of like-minded Christian women is life-giving to us radical homeschooling moms.

Whether you're just starting to think about educating your children at home or you're a veteran homeschooler, Mary Jo will help you wend through the maze of why, how, when, and where. She shares practical, realistic strategies for weaving learning into the tapestry of your family's life and shows you how to guide your children to be lifelong independent learners.

I hope every mom—whether single or married—will read "Solo Act," the insightful chapter about single parenting. It provides tremendous encouragement for single moms and wise advice for those who want to help them. A gift of this book could be a real blessing for a single homeschooling mom.

In nearly thirty years of reviewing books, I've never seen another book designed for the homeschooling mother who is also an entrepreneur. As the mother of five children with a large home business, I was often frustrated because no helps were available to me. I sometimes felt discouraged and alone. I wish I'd had this book back then! Ways to incorporate a home business into your family's life are woven throughout the book. The business chapter provides an excellent overview, yet it is detailed enough for experienced entrepreneurs to learn something new. And if you've never considered having a home business, it may open your eyes to some fascinating possibilities.

Stories help us relate to others and remember what we learn, and Mary Jo's stories add humor, richness, and reality to this book. Who will ever forget the lesson of honesty in her tale of the bloody manuscript and her need for an attitude adjustment about the delays in finishing this book? The inspiring examples of women who have studied under Mary Jo put flesh on her principles, demonstrating how others, too, can apply what they learn. What an encouragement!

And the quotes—oh, the quotes! How I love them. Excellent quotations can become guiding principles, and Mary Jo has enriched her book with some of the finest.

Even if you think you are too busy to do the suggested exercises at the end of each chapter, I urge you to make the time to work through them. By taking action on what you learn, you will increase the long-term benefits you'll gain from reading this book.

Remember, we are aiming toward the big picture—life management, not merely crisis management or even time management. Though you may feel overwhelmed and think your life is a shambles, through your awareness, admission, and working through *Flourish*, you are already beginning to make very positive changes.

Ask the Holy Spirit what He wants you to work on and in what order. He wants you to love, learn, and walk in truth—and He is the illuminator of truth. Trust Him!

TINA FAREWELL
www.BobandTinaFarewell.com

Acknowledgments

Just like living a flourishing life, writing a book requires a strong support network. I have been blessed with the best family, friends, and colleagues anyone could wish for, and I am grateful for them.

My sons—Forrest, Andrew, Perry, and Thomas—continually encourage, inspire, amuse, and amaze me. It's a privilege and a blessing to be their mother!

My parents, Jim and Rosemary Alinder, gave me a childhood overflowing with happy memories. They have always supported me in ways too countless to mention. Dad has stood in the gap for my boys and me during my years as a single mom, and Mom's death leaves a hole that can never be filled. I am forever grateful for their love.

Apologia's books have been part of my family's homeschool for many years, and I've been privileged to edit several of them. I'm thrilled to become an Apologia author, and I'm grateful for the support of such a strong publishing team. Davis Carman's visionary leadership is inspiring. Zan Tyler relentlessly encouraged me to write this book and discussed every chapter of the manuscript with me over the phone. Her wise editorial advice is priceless, but I treasure her friendship even more. Peggy Webb's diligence and thoroughness in checking facts and verifying quotations allowed me to focus my efforts on polishing the manuscript. It is challenging to edit an editor and humbling for an editor to be edited, and I am grateful for David Webb's fine-tuning. Doug Powell's cover design perfectly captured the beauty, warmth, and energy that distinguish a flourishing life, and Andrea Martin's lovely interior design complements it. Michelle Eichhorn's marketing savvy has been invaluable.

Bob and Tina Farewell's *Always Incomplete Resource Guide* played a huge part in my early homeschooling years. Their friendship, counsel, and encouragement have been a tremendous blessing. Tina read the working manuscript of *Flourish*, and I am so thankful for her helpful advice and for her foreword.

I am grateful to Kay Mitchell for sharing her story and for reviewing the chapters on single parenting and home business; to Mauricio Martinez and Carol Topp for their helpful suggestions on the home business chapter; and to Melissa Amaya, Raylene Hunt, Stephanie Kowalski-Gittings, Susie Leavitt, and Jennifer Rieth for their feedback on the single parent chapter.

Much of the material in this book is based on my "How Do You Do It All?" course, and the feedback of my students and coaching clients helped make the material even stronger. Their application of these principles in their own lives is inspiring. Special thanks to Lisa Barber, Stephanie Buckwalter, Dawn Clark, Joy Constant, Joy Hubbard, Kristen Johnson, Rita Johnson, Eleanor Joyce, Coleen Merk, Holly Nelson, Cathy Spain, Janet Wilfred, Melanie Young, and Robin in Texas for allowing me to share their stories.

Janet Wilfred has created most of my websites; her cheerful readiness to help and her friendship are a blessing. Robert Green's commitment to artistic excellence resonates in the graphics he designs for me, and he has been a helpful sounding board about business issues for many years.

My mastermind teammates and accountability partners have had a tremendous impact on my life, my family, and my business. Katherine Gowan, Louise Jones, Paula Seymour, Patti Thompson, Dawn Clark, Kristine Hall, Stevie Knight, Cathy Spain, Amy Pak, Felice Gerwitz, Maggie Hogan, and Kim Kautzer have kept me on track and blessed me with their friendship, wisdom, counsel, and encouragement.

Clay, Sally, and Joel Clarkson opened their lovely home in the Colorado mountains as a writing retreat while I was revising the first draft of this book. Phillip and Sandy Morris shared their lakeside cabin in the Mississippi woods while I reviewed the edited manuscript. What a blessing to hide away in such beautiful, peaceful settings to focus on my book!

Dr. Matthew J. Bruccoli helped me start my business and taught me most of what I know about writing, editing, book collecting, literature, and scholarship. There was no one else like him, and the world has been diminished by his death.

Rhea Perry helped me catch a vision for entrepreneurship and encouraged me to teach what I know. Mauricio Martinez frequently stepped on my toes with his astute coaching. Both Rhea and Mauricio pushed me ever farther out of my comfort zone and helped me grow my business.

During the darkest days of my life, five dear friends provided listening ears, shoulders to cry on, hugs, compassion, wise counsel, and lots of love. If only every single mom had friends like Rachel Green, Paula Shackelford, Polly Collum, Nell Hill, and Renée Jones! I can never thank them enough for being there for me. The members of Lawndale Presbyterian Church in Tupelo have blessed my family abundantly for many years and are a wonderful example of how believers can minister to single parents.

Nothing would be possible without the redeeming love, mercy, grace, and power of God. He has given me beauty for ashes (Isaiah 61:3) and satisfied my needs like a well-watered garden in a sun-scorched land (Isaiah 58:11). I thank Him and praise Him for His faithful providence in my life.

God shapes every second of our little lives
And minds every minute as the universe waits by.
The pain and the longing,
The joy and the moments of light
Are the rhythm and rhyme
The free verse of the poem of life.

MICHAEL CARD
"The Poem of Your Life"

CHAPTER 1

An Invitation to Flourish

Homeschool moms are hurting.

In recent years, I've asked hundreds of homeschooling moms about the biggest challenges they face, and their responses have been surprisingly similar. These women are deeply committed to their families and to educating their children at home, but they often feel overwhelmed.

How many of these challenges have you encountered in your own life?

- Becoming paralyzed by a to-do list so long that you don't know where to start

- Feeling guilty that you don't meet someone else's Supermom standards

- Dragging through each day exhausted and discouraged

- Finding it difficult to spend one-on-one time with each child

- Never having any "me" time—and feeling selfish for needing it

- Feeling so overwhelmed that you can't enjoy your family

- Neglecting your spiritual and physical health

- Saying yes when you really should say no

- Struggling to keep your house clean and your family's meals healthy

- Never having enough time or money

- Getting distracted and losing your focus

- Drowning in clutter so you can never find what you need

- Participating in extracurricular activities without overdoing it

- Constantly worrying that you're not getting enough done

- Having trouble setting priorities and staying motivated

- Feeling pulled in too many directions

You are not alone! Just like you, I've experienced every problem on this list. Yet through trial and error over many years, I've developed some powerful strategies to cut through the chaos and move toward a more balanced life. Now I want to share these strategies with you so that you can stop "just getting by" and flourish!

My Story

One of my goals for this book is to give glory to God for His work in my life. I want to share my story as a testimony to His faithfulness so that it may inspire hope in you and others. I see this as a way to redeem the struggles I've faced in my life by sharing what I've learned through those challenges.

Back at the turn of the millennium, I was a typical homeschooling mom, married with four sons. When my husband left me in early 2001 to live with another woman, I was shocked, angry, and scared. I was embarrassed to be divorced. For a while I felt as if a scarlet *D* were emblazoned on my dress. My sons—then ages 9, 6, 4, and 6 months—were bewildered, and their world was turned upside down. I was deeply committed to remaining at home with my children and continuing to homeschool them, yet I had no idea how I could support us all financially.

But God proved faithful. "A father to the fatherless, a defender of widows, is God in His holy dwelling" (Psalm 68:5). He has provided for all our needs through work I can do at home, help from my parents, and the loving ministry of a godly church.

Still, those early days were hard. For the first year, I received enough child support and alimony for us to live on. But then the child support dropped to zero for six months, and at one point I had to visit a local food pantry for groceries and assistance with that month's electric bill. That was the lowest point of my life.

It was clear that I was going to have to find a way to earn a living, so I turned to the skills I already had. I had written one book, *F. Scott Fitzgerald A to Z*, and I had done freelance editing off and on since 1986. I reconnected with my mentor from graduate school, and he began sending me some editing work. I didn't know much about running a business, but God providentially led me to some conferences for entrepreneurs where I began learning principles that could help me grow a home business while continuing to teach my children.

Grow, Know, and Go

The first event that I attended was Rhea Perry's Entrepreneur Days, a home business conference for homeschooling families. That was where I first began to get a vision for what was possible, to learn the things I needed to learn, and then eventually to take action. I call this process "Grow, know, and go." You grow by getting vision and seeing the possibilities for your life. You know by obtaining education, learning new things, and meeting people who can help you. The last and most important step is go. You must take action on what you've learned and build on it. Only then will any real progress occur.

> There are two sure ways to fail: Think and never do, or do and never think.
> ZIG ZIGLAR

As I began applying what I learned, my freelance editing business gradually shifted from sporadic to steady to overflowing. Because of the upheaval in my life, I took several years to move through the steps of grow, know, and go.

It wasn't just about the money; it was also about our life as a family. I wanted *financial freedom*—to take care of the bills and rid myself of the terrible looming pressure of not knowing where the next bag of groceries was coming from—but I also wanted *time freedom*. I wanted time to spend with my boys. I wanted time to minister to other people. I wanted time to take care of myself and my own health without collapsing physically and burning out emotionally.

Get Out of Your Comfort Zone

One of the most important strategies you can employ to achieve balance and gain financial freedom and time freedom is moving out of your comfort zone. Getting out of your comfort zone is, well, uncomfortable! But it's absolutely essential if you're going to experience growth and success. I learned this lesson in a rather surprising way.

My second son, Andrew, went with me to a home business conference in Phoenix when he was ten. Just a year before, he had been uncomfortable shaking hands and looking an adult in the eye. He really grew at that conference, as I urged him (OK, I pushed him) to get out of his comfort zone. He gave a sales pitch with a handheld microphone in front of 200 people and won a contest to raise money for charity.

After the conference we visited the Grand Canyon. It was utterly glorious! Andrew is a bit more adventurous than I am, so he walked right up to the edge of the Grand Canyon and stood near the guide, who was dangling her legs over the side. But I kept further back because I don't particularly care for heights. Actually, I'm scared of heights. Terrified.

> One must from time to time attempt things that are beyond one's capacity.
> AUGUSTE RENOIR

So Andrew challenged me. "You know, Mom, if I could get out of my comfort zone enough to speak in front of two hundred strangers, I think you could get out of your comfort zone by moving a little closer to the edge of the Grand Canyon, couldn't you?"

That trip to Arizona triggered massive action and progress for me. The first thing that I did was to stop. I cut out several of my least profitable business endeavors, including some activities I enjoyed that were not the best use of my time. I also raised my rates to reflect the value of my experience and expertise and referred simpler projects to other editors. At one point, I even hired someone to edit the new material I wrote for an expanded version of my own book—a huge step for a perfectionist like me! I gradually expanded my services to include book coaching and collaborative writing. Perhaps most importantly, I began to teach what I knew. People often ask me how to start their own freelance editing business, so I taught a class on editing and developed it into a home-study course.

> What you can do, or dream you can, begin it. Boldness has genius, power, and magic in it.
> JOHN ANSTER's translation of Goethe's *Faust*

Over the next year, I doubled my income and won a contest for the most-improved business. I'm still enjoying the laptop computer I won, but the most valuable part of the contest was that it forced me to think seriously and strategically about where I wanted my business to go, where the money was going to come from, and what I wanted my family life to look like. That's when I began developing and refining the principles and strategies in this book.

I encourage you to think about how you can get outside your own comfort zone and begin to grow and flourish. This book will provide you with helpful guidance and encouragement along the way.

Flourish!

What exactly does it mean to flourish? It means to grow vigorously, luxuriate, be revived, or abound. It can also mean making dramatic gestures or adding a creative touch, such as a trumpet fanfare or an embellishment in writing or decorating. The overarching ideas are thriving and abundance.

When we get bogged down in the difficulties and challenges of our busy lives, we start drooping like a wilted plant that hasn't been watered in a long time. But it's the flourishing plant—one that has been well tended, with the right balance of good soil, water, and light—that grows and offers beauty or nourishment. When you are flourishing, you can take better care of your family so that they too will flourish.

> The LORD will guide you always; he will satisfy your needs in a sun-scorched land and will strengthen your frame. You will be like a well-watered garden, like a spring whose waters never fail.
>
> ISAIAH 58:11 (NIV)

About This Book

This book first began to take shape with a teleseminar I taught called "How Do You Do It All? Proven Strategies for Balancing Family Life and Home Business in the Real World." Since 2007, this seminar has been available as a downloadable home study course, and the feedback I've received from my students and coaching clients has helped me refine my system further.

One of the reasons I wanted to teach that class and write this book is that I couldn't find anybody who is really addressing the practical issues involved in balancing homeschooling, family life, and a home business. There are a lot of wonderful time-management and productivity systems for business people, but they generally ignore the existence of family responsibilities. Many are designed for people who spend most of their time in an office and don't have to deal with fussy babies, hungry toddlers, energetic grade-schoolers, and busy teenagers. Books written for corporate jet-setters just don't speak to moms like me.

On the other hand, there are some wonderful homemaking guides and planners for moms at home—including some designed particularly for homeschoolers—but they usually don't accommodate a home business. Have you ever looked at a sample schedule in one of those books and thought, "Well, that looks great, but where do I find time to earn a living?" Even if you don't have a home business, some of those books can be intimidating because they seem to be promoting an unattainable standard.

Let's get this out of the way now: I am not Supermom. I've personally test-driven a lot of mistakes, so maybe you can learn from my experience. I'm going to tell it to you straight—the good, the bad, *and* the ugly. I always want to be realistic—I want to offer you an attainable standard while providing you encouragement, inspiration, and motivation.

Ultimately, everything depends on God. His strength is sufficient for me and you:

> And He has said to me, "My grace is sufficient for you, for power is perfected in weakness." Most gladly, therefore, I will rather boast about my weaknesses, so that the power of Christ may dwell in me. (2 Corinthians 12:9)

The personal stories I'll be sharing in these pages are not really about me. They're about how God has worked in my life and the principles I've learned that I've been able to apply through His power. Don't just implement the strategies I'm teaching. I urge you to rely on God and on His power in your life.

I'm dropping so many balls, I'm in danger of getting a concussion! Our friends call us dynamos, but we feel more like broken-down lawnmowers coughing and choking through the day and constantly having to be restarted. Or like somebody trying to put out a forest fire with a damp cloth. One of us, me or the fire, is going to get beaten to death! By bedtime, I'm thinking of a quote from *The Little Engine That Could*, "I must rest my weary wheels."
MELANIE YOUNG, North Carolina

Adjust These Strategies to Fit Your Life

Jesus taught in parables because stories convey truth in a powerful way. The principles are the skeleton, and the stories of how they work out in real life are the flesh on the bones. They work together to give us a complete picture. You'll find many stories and real-life examples in this book. In addition to my own experiences, I will share stories from moms who've taken the "How Do You Do It All?" course that provided the foundation for this book.

I'm going to be making lots of suggestions and telling you about strategies that work well for me and my family, as well as my students and coaching clients. *But there is no one right way to do most of these things.* Take what you read here and adjust the principles to fit your own lifestyle. Test them, tweak them, and refine them. Pray to discern which are important for your family's life.

For example, I talk a lot about home business because that's a big part of my family's life and the life of many other homeschooling families. Even if you don't have a home business, I encourage you not to skip these parts of the book. You'll find principles and strategies that you can apply to other areas of your life. Also, the recent economy has forced a lot of people to figure out how to make money at home. If your financial circumstances change, you may someday consider starting a home business, in which case you'll have a head start. Joy Hubbard, a Mississippi mom, told me, "I know necessity creates motivation. I really don't have a burning desire to start my own knitting business because I have a very comfortable life now. But things could change, and you've provided me the steps to do it."

Likewise, I'm a single mom, and I have included some examples specifically meant to encourage single moms. Most of you are married, but I suggest you read these stories. You will find principles to apply to your own life, and you may find inspiration for helping the single moms you know. Take it from me: They need you!

> The important thing is generally the "next step." We ought not to take it unless we are sure that it is advisable; but we should not hesitate to take it once we *are* sure; and we can safely join with others who also wish to take it, without bothering our heads overmuch as to any fantastic theories they may have concerning, say, the two hundredth step, which is not yet in sight.
>
> THEODORE ROOSEVELT

I am also writing to moms as individuals, but those of you who are married will want to do some of the exercises in this book both individually and in partnership with your husband.

So if you read something in these pages that's not a perfect fit for where you are right now, find a different way to apply that principle in your own life.

Furthermore, you may notice what appear to be several contradictions as you read this book. For example, I am going to talk about multitasking, but I'm also going to talk about focusing. I'm going to talk about developing a routine, but I'm also going to talk about being flexible. I'm going to talk about thinking big, but I'm also going to talk about being realistic. I'm going to urge you not to waste your time, but I'm also going to encourage you to take time to stop and smell the roses. Such advice may appear contradictory at first glance, yet learning which strategy to apply in each situation is part of finding balance in a flourishing life.

Apply What You Learn

At the end of each chapter you will find one or more activities to help you take action and apply what you've learned in these pages. Write your reflections on these activities to record your growth and gain the most from this book.

Choose a journal, notebook, or three-ring binder just for these exercises. You might even use your creativity to decorate it. Customizable forms for some of the activities are provided at www. FlourishAtHome.com/book. If you choose to use these, a three-ring binder will probably work best.

Some of the activities will be challenging. I am going to encourage you to ask yourself some hard questions. I understand it's likely that the whole reason you're reading this book is that you need more time. You're not looking for *more* things to do to fill your time; you're hoping to streamline your life. But doing these exercises can have a profound impact on your life, family, productivity, and (if applicable) business that will more than repay the effort. If you were already satisfied with the way that everything is working for you now, you probably wouldn't be reading this book. If you're not completely satisfied with your life on a daily basis, then face it—you're going to have to make some changes. And that's what I hope to help you do.

Take Action!

❏ Before you move on to the next chapter, take some time to complete the Pre-Book Self-Evaluation in appendix B. This will help you identify the challenges you currently face and get the most benefit from the rest of the book. It will also give you a way to measure your progress after you finish the book and activities.

CHAPTER 2

Change Your Mind to Change Your Time

We always have time enough, if we will but use it aright.
JOHANN WOLFGANG VON GOETHE

"How do you *do* it all?" That's a question every homeschool mom faces every day. For me, the short answer to that question is this: I don't, and I redefine "it all."

In many ways, these two little statements sum up this entire book in a nutshell. Nearly every strategy I share here can fit somewhere under these two categories: I don't, and I redefine "it all."

Nobody does it all. In order to flourish—to restore balance to a busy life—we have to start by changing our mindset. In this chapter we'll explore ways to change your mindset to help you redefine "it all."

Stop Struggling with Juggling

Have you ever talked about the difficulty of juggling all your responsibilities? It's a common metaphor, and I used it for many years. You have all these "balls" that you're juggling, and it's so hard to keep everything in the air. I finally realized that the juggling act inevitably leads to dropping the ball.

When you're caught up in the juggling act, you tend to think in terms of crisis management, which results in a triage approach to life. Triage is a medical strategy for dividing battle or disaster victims into three categories: those who are going to die anyway no matter what you do for them, those who are going to survive anyway no matter what you do for them, and the group in the middle who are going to die without help but might survive if you help them. It's this last group that receives top-priority attention. When you take the triage approach to life, you tend to ignore the things that aren't going to get done no matter what, ignore the things that will be taken care of anyway, and give all your attention to the crisis. It's the tyranny of the urgent.

As a newly single mom, triage quickly became my default approach to life. When I was working on an editing deadline, I tended to spend less time with my kids and taking care of the house. When I didn't have a paying project, I would neglect my business (I hadn't yet learned about marketing) and spend extra time reading to the boys, working on their homeschool lessons, and cleaning the house. When a new editing project came in, I'd shift my attention back to business. I often told my children, "If I can just get past this one deadline, when I finish this editing job, things will be different." And I believed what

I was saying. I wasn't lying to them; I was fooling myself.

You just can't live that way very long. Life is a marathon, not a sprint. You have to find a pace that you can maintain over the long haul. Operating in overdrive until you get past "just one more deadline" and rushing frantically from one crisis to the next is simply not sustainable. You *will* burn out—and that's not going to be good for anybody.

> My life was/is in triage mode, and I feel burnt out. It isn't anything new, but I'm a driven Type A, and it's hard not to try and do it all. Saying no is the single most important strategy I've learned.
> RITA JOHNSON, Illinois

Triage is not a long-term strategy for daily living; triage is a strategy for emergencies. If you are constantly operating in triage mode, that's a sign your life is like a disaster scene.

Here's a great example of what my life was like when I was living in constant triage. This is a letter I sent to two of my editing clients in August 2005, just before my trip to the Grand Canyon. I'm not usually quite this transparent with my clients, but they were young men with an interesting sense of humor, so I figured they would be able to appreciate the Rube Goldberg-esque nature of the incident:

> If you see any blood on the manuscript, it's from cutting my thumb while picking up pieces of the toilet tank lid, which broke when it fell off the trash can, where I'd set it hastily while trying unsuccessfully to prevent the clogged toilet from overflowing while the phone was ringing with a message from another client just as I was copying the last few pages of your book, trying to get to FedEx in time to

get it to you tomorrow, so you might have a shot at getting it ready for the California homeschool convention, and hopefully then I would get to the Boy Scout store before it closed to buy a Webelo manual for my ten-year-old son who is joining Cub Scouts tonight so that he will be eligible for this weekend's Camporee with an opportunity to fly in a real airplane because he wants to be a rocket scientist. I applied an economy-brand bandage, but the blood soaked through the teeny little pad as I was packing your manuscript into the envelope. Buy Band-Aid brand.

Balance Is Not a Myth

Eventually I realized there's a much better metaphor than juggling for what I wanted to accomplish: tightrope walking. Tightrope walkers make frequent small adjustments to maintain their balance. They lean a little to the right and a little to the left, adjusting gradually without big sudden shifts. That image of maintaining balance rather than juggling made a powerful difference in the way I approached my daily life.

When you catch yourself saying, "I've got so much to juggle" or "I can't keep all these balls in the air," stop and think about dropping the balls, scattering them all over the floor, and tripping on them. Then call the image of a tightrope walker to mind and begin thinking in terms

> Biblical balance is more practical than pragmatism. It is more thoughtful than rationalism. It is more experienced than existentialism and more romantic than sentimentalism. It is more stable than conservatism and more progressive than liberalism.
>
> DR. GEORGE GRANT
> *The Micah Mandate*

of balance. You may be surprised at what a difference this simple shift in your mindset makes.

Several years after I first thought of the tightrope analogy, I watched Nik Wallenda cross Niagara Falls (and, later, the Grand Canyon) on a wire, praying aloud all the way. This was both terrifying and inspiring. I was fascinated by Wallenda's description of how he uses the balance pole as an extension of his arms to adjust to changing conditions, such as a gust of wind. If there's too much bounce in the cable, he kneels until it stabilizes. This is a great reminder that we too must adjust to changing conditions to maintain balance in our lives.

Some people disparage the idea of life balance as a myth, but most of these critics have a very narrow view of balance, as if it requires keeping all the wedges exactly the same size in the pie chart of life. That would indeed be impossible. To look at it another way, if you were weighing feathers against rocks on an old-fashioned balance scale, putting an equal number of feathers on one side and rocks on the other would not create balance. To balance the scale, you'd have to use vastly different numbers of feathers and rocks. If someone suddenly dropped an orange in among the feathers, you'd have to remove some rocks to keep things balanced. If you needed to measure other objects, such as pennies or marshmallows, the quantities would change again.

True balance doesn't mean spending an equal amount of time and attention on each area of your life. It means spending an *appropriate* amount of time and attention on each area. Just like walking on the high wire, balancing your life involves responding wisely to changing conditions. Sometimes you have to shift your attention from one area to another. Other times you have to stop and rest until things calm down a bit. Unlike the drastic disparities of the triage approach, these gradual, ongoing adjustments will help you maintain your long-term balance.

Evaluate the Circumstances of Your Life

When you hear someone talking about balance, it's easy to think, "Well, yeah, but she doesn't have my challenges" or "My situation is different." Well, that's true: Your life is different from everybody else's. Each of us has unique circumstances, and that's why I emphasize adjusting and modifying my principles to fit your situation.

Although the details of our circumstances vary greatly, they mostly fall into three main categories:

1. **Irreducible Facts.** The first group of circumstances includes things you *can't* change. These are things you really can't do anything about, at least not right away. My irreducible fact is that I'm a single mom with four children. If you're struggling with chronic illness, that's your irreducible fact. Or you may be caring for a sick spouse or an aging parent. These are the circumstances of your life that everything else has to fit around.

2. **Non-Negotiables.** Then there are the things that you *won't* change. For example, two non-negotiables for me are that I will homeschool my children and I will build my business at home rather than leaving my children to take a job outside the home. Everything else has to fit with these circumstances.

3. **Preferences.** If irreducible facts and non-negotiables were all we had, there wouldn't be much we could do to effect change in our lives. Fortunately there is a third category. These are the things you *can* change and are *willing* to change. I call these preferences. Preferences are not unimportant, but this is where the wiggle room is. This is where you have the opportunity to negotiate

and compromise. An example of a preference I've had to compromise is that I really like having a flexible schedule and designing my own educational program, but I've chosen to participate in a rigorous homeschool co-op because the benefits outweigh the reduced flexibility.

The three kinds of circumstances helped me to identify and prioritize what must stay and what got booted. . . . Since I can't change the facts, I changed my attitude toward them, and that was extremely beneficial.
LISA BARBER, Mississippi

Find Peace in the Space Between the Ideal and Reality

One of my most important rules is "No Whining." The irreducible facts are just that—facts. Pity parties are simply counterproductive, and they sap your energy. The cure for whining is one of my most fundamental principles:

Find peace in the space between the ideal and reality.

The ideal is what you would be doing and what you would have if you could do and have anything you want without any complications or the hindrances of ordinary life. The reality is your everyday life—the facts you have to deal with. The question is: What are you going to do in the middle?

Some people don't like the word *compromise* because they think it means somehow undermining their principles. You shouldn't have to sacrifice your principles or ignore your priorities. The solution is compromising on how your priorities play out practically. You will always have to make choices.

> I am a woman of strong passion and conviction. With that comes a lack of flexibility at times. You would think that divorce, three special-needs kids, chronic pain, and a sleep disorder would have forced me to compromise. I'm finally realizing how much stress I make for myself internally when I try to realize the unreal. Learning that I need to deal with life on life's terms, and not according to some *Better Homes and Gardens* article from the fifties, has really helped me.
> HOLLY NELSON, Kansas

For example, one of my preferences is reading aloud. I would love to read aloud to my children two hours every evening, all snuggled up together on the sofa in front of a blazing fire. Sounds wonderful, doesn't it? We enjoyed many leisurely read-aloud times when my boys were younger, but that's just not a realistic goal for our lives right now. However, that doesn't mean that I throw reading aloud completely out the window. What it does mean is that instead of reading together every day, perhaps we do it one afternoon or evening a week. Or maybe we listen to an audiobook while folding laundry or riding in the car. Sometimes an older child will read aloud to a younger child. All of these are different ways to get the same benefits of reading aloud together or hearing great literature even though I can't always have my ideal of snuggling up on the sofa, and I've found peace with these alternatives.

Don't let the simplicity of this principle fool you. It's disarmingly powerful. Dawn Clark, one of my coaching clients, found it's made a big difference in her life:

By accepting that which doesn't match up to my ideal, I can pour my energies into being a woman of motion rather than being paralyzed by my list of what "should be" but isn't. No longer do I have my eyes on the disappointments of what I'm not doing. Instead, I can now focus on the potential opportunities of what can be done.

Think in Terms of Life Management, Not Time Management

Change the way you think and talk about time. How often have you said, "I just don't have time for this"? Instead of "I don't have time," train yourself to ask, "How can I make time for it?" Phrasing the problem as a question opens your mind to other possibilities and reminds you that you have a choice about how you spend your time. You also need to consider whether you *should* make time for the activity in question.

Of course, we don't actually *make* time. Rather, we decide how to allocate the time we've been given. Perhaps you feel like you don't have any control over how you use your time. But think about times when you have been super-productive.

> When you say, "I don't have time for this task," you really mean, "I don't consider it as important as something else I want or need to do." For whatever reason, you have decided to use the hours another way. The issue is not lack of time but a choice you have made.
> CHARLES HUMMEL
> *Freedom from Tyranny of the Urgent*

Most people get more done in the day just before a vacation or business trip than they usually do in two or three regular days. High motivation and an immovable deadline can spur us into overdrive. Or consider how you immediately drop everything you have planned—no matter how important—when there's an accident, illness, or death in the family. Last year, I spent a day in the emergency room when my oldest son was in a car wreck. A month later, I spent another day in the ER when my father experienced heart trouble and then had a pacemaker implanted. Suddenly, schedules, plans, and deadlines didn't matter at all.

As you've seen, you can't live permanently in crisis mode, but these examples demonstrate how you *can* choose to make time for whatever matters to you. You'll find a lot of discussion about time in this book, but don't think primarily in terms of time management. Instead, think in terms of *life* management—that is, balancing all of life in the real world so that you and your family can flourish.

Take Action!

❒ Are you caught up in the juggling act? How will learning to balance your life better make a difference to you and your family?

❒ Identify the three types of circumstances in your own life:

1. Irreducible facts—what you can't change

2. Non-negotiables—what you won't change

3. Preferences—what you can and will change

❒ What is your ideal? What is your reality? How will you begin to find peace in the space between the ideal and reality?

❒ Start shifting the way you think and talk about time. Instead of saying "I don't have time for this," train yourself to ask "How can I make time for this?"

CHAPTER 3

The Freedom Toolbox

*If you really want to do something, you'll find a way;
if you don't, you'll find an excuse.*
JIM ROHN, Personal achievement philosopher

We've talked about changing your mindset. Now we shift to changing your behavior. FREEDOM is an acronym I use for remembering seven important strategies for meeting all of the various challenges and obligations of life:

Focus	**D**iscipline
Reflect	**O**rganize
Educate	**M**ultitask
Eliminate	

Focus

The F in FREEDOM stands for *focus*. Spend some time thinking about what it is that only you can do, and then prioritize those things.

There are lots of things *anybody* can do, including you, and there are some things *only you* can do. For example, only you can nurse your baby, but someone else can change diapers. Only you can write your book (unless you hire a ghostwriter), but someone else can process and ship orders.

In addition to considering what only you can do, think about what only you *should* do, what matters more to you than it does to anyone else, and what you do better than anyone else could. As a homeschool mom, you've made educating your own children a priority instead of delegating their education to an institution. Most other things have to take second place to that focus.

> Things that matter most must never be at the mercy of things that matter least.
> JOHANN WOLFGANG VON GOETHE

We'll be looking at ways to delegate some tasks, but the fact that something can be delegated doesn't necessarily mean that it *should*. That's why it's so important to begin by identifying your priorities and focusing on them.

If you have a home business, that will be another high priority. If you're just getting started, or if you're trying to improve your current business, you need to find a focus for your business. What are you passionate about? What are your most profitable skills? What is unique about what you have to offer? What jobs are important for you to handle personally?

In his book *Good to Great*, Jim Collins introduces what he calls "the hedgehog concept" to help choose your focus in the overlap among three circles. (The hedgehog concept is based on an ancient Greek proverb that says the fox knows many things, but the hedgehog knows one big thing.) The first circle is what you can be the best in the world at. If that sounds a little too ambitious, what can you be the best at in your field? What can you be the best at in your country? What can you be the best at in your community? What are you really gifted at? What is the skill where you really excel? The second circle is what you are deeply passionate about. Even if you're good at it, if you don't care about it, then you're going to burn out quickly. The third circle is what drives your economic engine—how your business will make money.

Even if you never start a business, you can apply the hedgehog concept to your family. What are your gifts and talents and those of your family? What are you deeply passionate about? (This might include an area of ministry or service.) How will you be a good steward of the gifts, talents, and money God has given you? What should you focus on?

Reflect

The R in FREEDOM stands for *reflect*. Zig Ziglar's admonition bears repeating: Two sure ways to fail are to think and never do, and do but never think.

It's important to take action, but action must be founded on reflection. Taking time to reflect forces you to be honest with yourself, so it helps you find your focus, identify what you should do, set appropriate goals to match your priorities, and evaluate how well you are accomplishing those goals. In chapter 5, we'll look at guidelines for setting goals; in chapter 6, we'll explore seven tools for planning how to achieve your goals.

Don't be afraid to ask yourself tough questions. If this is hard for you, you may need a friend, coach, or accountability partner to help you. It's easy to be blind to things in your own life that someone else can readily see in you. When coaching moms one on one, I sometimes realize I need to remind myself of the advice I'm giving them!

Reflection requires quiet time and solitude so you can think clearly without interruption. If you have very young children or very many children, you may be laughing or rolling your eyes at this point. It's hard. I'm not denying that. It's not easy to set aside quiet time or find a place to be alone. Frankly, I get a lot of my best ideas in the shower—it's the one place where nobody can interrupt me! Take whatever opportunity you can find to think and reflect. Keep pen and paper handy (in your purse, in the kitchen, on your nightstand . . . well, not in the shower) so that you can jot down brainstorms as they come.

Making time for reflection is increasingly rare in our noisy, busy world. However, as missionary Jim Elliot pointed out, there's a spiritual aspect to the need for quiet time:

> I think the devil has made it his business to monopolize on three elements: noise, hurry, crowds. If he can keep us hearing radios, gossip, conversation, or even sermons, he is happy. But he will not allow quietness. . . . Let us resist the devil in this by avoiding noise as much as we can, purposefully seeking to spend time alone, facing ourselves in the Word. . . . Satan is aware of where we find our strength. May he not rob us![1]

Educate

The first E in FREEDOM stands for *educate*. When my son Andrew was nine, he asked me why I keep going to conferences. I told him I want to learn new things. With a mixture of shock and alarm, he replied, "You mean you're not fully educated yet?" It was a great opportunity to explain that we should never stop learning and growing. At the age of eighty-seven, Michelangelo reportedly said, "*Ancora imparo*," which means "I am still learning." What an inspiring example!

It's easy to get so caught up in educating your children that you forget about educating yourself. You need to expose yourself to new ideas and new methods on a regular basis for all three life areas—personal, family, and business. Continually sharpen your skills and broaden your mind. Learn new ideas and methods for educating your children and running your household. Discover new ways to build your business. Educating yourself is part of operating a business. Don't think you're not working when you're learning new things. Just don't let education become an excuse for avoiding action.

> Read at every wait; read at all hours; read within leisure; read in times of labor; read as one goes in; read as one goes out. The task of the educated mind is simply put: read to lead.
> CICERO

One mom recently told me she would really like to have an hour a day to read. I encouraged her to find a way to make it happen. Depending on your circumstances, an hour a day may seem like an impossible dream or it may seem like not nearly enough. Find a way to make learning a regular part of your life through one of the many formats available these days—books, magazines, live conferences, teleseminars, webinars, podcasts, audios, videos, or home study courses.

To help you implement what you learn, take notes on what you read or hear (unless you're driving!). Feel free to mark your books as you read. I underline important passages, write captions at the tops of the pages, argue with authors in the margins, create my own topical index in the front or back, and put a star by favorite quotations. Discuss what you've read with your family and friends. Sharing what you've studied is an important part of the learning process.

If you want your children to value reading, they need to see *you* reading—for pleasure as well as for learning. I'm a lifelong bibliophile, so our house is filled to overflowing with books. We have forty-nine bookcases at last count. I keep a written record of every book I've read since I graduated from college. If you're a fellow book lover, I invite you to visit my blog at www. EclecticBibliophile.com.

Eliminate

The second E in FREEDOM stands for *eliminate*. Make time for what you need to focus on by eliminating activities that don't fit your goals and priorities. We'll concentrate on activities here, but you can also learn to eliminate counterproductive mindsets (chapter 2), bad attitudes (chapter 8), and "stuff" (chapter 12).

You can eliminate some activities by never beginning them in the first place (just say no!) or by stopping them if you're already involved. As we'll see in chapter 7, other people will respect your time only as far as you value and respect it yourself.

Saying no can be very challenging. I understand you don't want to let other people down. But not everything that needs to be done is something *you* need to do. Opportunity does not equal obligation. Seek God's guidance and evaluate every opportunity in light of your goals and your priorities. Remember that saying yes to one thing means saying no to everything else at the same time. Sometimes you need to say no to a good thing in order to say yes to something even better.

Elisabeth Elliot offers this wise counsel: "If we really have too much to do, there are some items on the agenda that God did not put there. Let us submit the list to Him and ask Him to indicate which items we must delete. There is always time to do the will of God. If we are too busy to do that, we are too busy."[2]

One day I had an opportunity to say no twice within ten minutes. A friend asked me to teach a poetry class for a girls' activity group. I love teaching a weekly literature class to high school students in our homeschool co-op, but teaching an extra class to another group just didn't fit with my priorities. She could find someone else to teach poetry, or she could offer another subject. I said no without feeling guilty about it.

As soon as I hung up the phone, I got a call from another friend who was going to be in town getting her tires rotated. She had a couple of hours to kill and wanted to hang out together. However, I had scheduled a call with a client, so I had to say no. Having fun with friends is important to me, and another time I would gladly have gotten together with her. Looking back, I realize that I felt more comfortable saying no because I had a specific time conflict—a coaching call—than I would have if I'd simply had a busy day planned. To be true to what I teach, I should have been able to say just as comfortably, "I'm sorry. I'm not free today, but I'd love to get together another time."

In addition to stopping and saying no to things, you can also choose to delegate or outsource. Delegating and outsourcing are two ways to accomplish the same goal: getting someone else to do a task so that you can focus on your priorities. For example, you can delegate almost all household tasks to your children (see chapter 12). Participating in a homeschool co-op is one way to delegate part of your children's education while you retain primary responsibility for it (see chapter 13). You can also delegate interruptions by letting an answering machine or voice mail take messages.

Outsourcing goes a step beyond delegating by paying other people to do specific tasks such as lawn care, housecleaning, piano lessons, math tutoring, or running errands. If you have a business, consider the hourly value of your own time—many tasks can be outsourced inexpensively so that you can concentrate on creative and income-producing activities. For example, you can outsource the processing and shipping of orders, duplicating audio CDs, accounting, keyword research, website design, and much more.

In chapter 6, you'll learn how to create a Stop-Doing List to help you eliminate lower-priority activities from your life.

> I've found freedom to stop doing some things and energy to put into my family. I'm a doer and guilty of doing without thinking. Now I'm finding balance in thinking before just jumping in and doing.
> RITA JOHNSON, Illinois

Discipline

D stands for *discipline*—self-discipline, that is. Self-discipline is an essential tool for homeschool moms. Freedom and flexibility are wonderful aspects of homeschooling, but without an external accountability system in place, it's easy to abuse that freedom.

Self-discipline is essential, if tough, for entrepreneurs as well because, after all, freedom to do things your own way, on your own schedule, is a major part of the attraction of working from home. Without the built-in accountability of reporting to an employer, you must be diligent and avoid the temptation to abuse your freedom. I'm speaking from experience. There was a time when I was so caught up in the excitement of being free and flexible in running my own business that I didn't work as hard as I could and should have.

Here's an example of what can happen when you lose focus and don't practice self-discipline. One of the biggest—and potentially most profitable—projects I have ever undertaken turned into a disaster. The client was demanding and hard to get along with. I spent a lot of time avoiding the project and, I must confess, I spent a lot of time whining about it. When I reviewed my time log for the project, I was ashamed when I realized just how few hours I had actually spent on it. Because the project was such a psychological burden, it seemed like it had consumed my life. But when I looked at the cold, hard facts, I realized I had spent more time avoiding and whining about it than I had actually working on it. After that rude awakening, I disciplined myself to finish it and move on to the next thing to avoid making the same mistake in the future.

> Self-discipline is the ability to make yourself do something you don't necessarily want to do, to get a result you would really like to have.
>
> ANDY ANDREWS

I find this admonition from Brady Boyd quite convicting:

What is the use of a teacher who doesn't teach, a writer who doesn't write, a painter who doesn't paint, an investor who doesn't invest, a pastor who doesn't pastor, a leader who doesn't lead—and a sports team that can't play the sport? Whatever it is we are called to do, we are called to do it as unto God. Sloppiness and laziness and an undisciplined life do *nothing* to honor him. Instead we are to grow and develop and improve and work hard, knowing it is our excellence that points glory his way. He has given us resources to steward— time, talent, money, smarts—and he is a fan of stewardship that is wise.[3]

Self-discipline is necessary to do what you know need to do, whether it involves homeschooling, home business, helping someone else, or taking care of yourself. Plan your priorities, and then take action on them. Work efficiently. Meet challenges with action, not avoidance.

Organize

The O in FREEDOM stands for *organize*. Organization is self-discipline applied in an orderly way to free you to focus on what's most important. How organized you are has a tremendous impact on the atmosphere of your home. Disorganization creates chaos, while organization promotes peace. Which do you prefer?

If one aspect of your life is unorganized, it has a spillover effect on every other aspect of your life. For example, if you can't find your car keys, you'll become flustered and you may be late for church. If you're sleep-deprived or running late, you're much likelier to forget things and drop things, which will make you even later. If you don't keep your pantry stocked, you'll have to battle the crowds doing panic shopping when a blizzard or hurricane is forecast, spending more time, money, and energy than you would have if you'd planned ahead.

On the other hand, if you discipline yourself to organize your time, tasks, thoughts, and things, your life will go more smoothly, even during hard times. Organization promotes efficiency, productivity, sanity, peace, and freedom.

Organization even affects our relationships. If you're late or frazzled, you may become irritated and

> Reduce all your worldly business, your affairs, your property, your domains, your employments, your pleasures—reduce *every-thing to order*. Without it, you cannot have a peaceful mind, and of course, cannot be happy.
> JACOB ABBOTT
> *The Way to Do Good*

impatient with your family. As Marilyn Rockett explains, "People are more important than things, but things out of control hinder our relationships with people."[4] Recently, I was annoyed because couldn't find my Crocs when I was in a hurry to check the mail on a cold, wet day. I interrogated each of my boys, certain that one of them had borrowed my shoes (again) and failed to return them to their usual place in the kitchen. They all pled innocent. Imagine my chagrin when I found them—under my desk, where I had kicked them off several hours earlier. I apologized rather sheepishly, and we laughed at my forgetfulness.

There's no one right way to organize. Professional organizer Stephanie Winston reminds us, "Order is not an end in itself. Order is whatever helps you to function effectively—nothing more and nothing less."[5] Examine your life to identify areas in which you're not functioning effectively and commit to becoming more organized. Creating order takes longer and is harder than maintaining order, but it's well worth the effort.

In chapter 6, we'll discuss seven planning tools to help you organize your tasks and time. In chapter 12, we'll look at strategies for organizing your things—the stuff that can quickly explode into chaos if you don't keep it under control.

Multitask

Finally, the M in FREEDOM stands for *multitask*. We started this chapter with focusing, and we're ending with multitasking. Sounds contradictory? Well, it's not. The challenge is that you have to figure out when to focus on a single task and when to multitask.

In recent years it's become popular to condemn multitasking. Some say that if you can multitask while you are doing something, it's not worth your time. In business, this might indicate tasks you can outsource. A bigger concern is that multitasking undermines focus and is therefore inefficient. Those who say this, however, are speaking almost exclusively of *mental* multitasking—usually the digital distractions presented by computers and smartphones. Students who play games, check e-mail, or use social media in the classroom or while studying are definitely diluting their concentration and learning much less than if they focused all their attention on the lesson. Likewise, in the workplace, people who constantly check e-mail and use social media are less efficient.

I need to walk on the treadmill for my health, but it was always such a chore for me until I realized I could multitask while doing it. I began listening to opera and classical music while walking, and later I started reading as well. I didn't want to waste my time on just anything; I wanted to go a step further with books that I wouldn't normally read, such as *Brave New World* and Margaret Thatcher's *Path to Power*. Instead of miserably looking at the timer while I walked, reading and listening to music gave me pleasure and helped me stick to it.

JOY HUBBARD, Mississippi

Combining two mental tasks clearly doesn't work, but that's not what I'm advocating. Rather, I'm suggesting you look for ways to combine physical tasks with lighter mental tasks. Used judiciously, this kind of multitasking can buy you time to focus on your priorities. It helps you do more with your twenty-four hours and trains you to use small blocks of time efficiently. As organizing expert Eileen Roth says, "I sincerely believe that you can only do one thing at a time well, but how well do you need to wait in line?"[6]

Fold a load of laundry or empty the dishwasher while you're talking on the phone. Talk on your cell phone with a friend or accountability partner while you're walking. Or use that quiet time to be alone with your thoughts or in prayer. Listen to books on tape or educational CDs while you're driving in the car or walking for exercise. I've listened to everything from Homer's *Odyssey* to William Zinsser's *On Writing Well* while driving or walking. Of course, the hitch is that you can't take notes while you're driving, but you can still absorb some of the information, discern the big idea, and jot down notes when you reach your destination.

Introducing new math concepts requires focus, but you can quiz your child on multiplication facts or spelling words while you're preparing dinner. Look for opportunities to teach impromptu lessons. While waiting endlessly at the emergency room with one of my children on a weekend, we had a little lesson in Business 101. We talked about how he could set up a business and the importance of finding customers. (You'll find this story in chapter 13.) I worked on organizing the chapters and topics of this book while waiting at the hospital during my dad's outpatient surgery.

Closely related to multitasking is using small blocks of time efficiently. Keep a book or a magazine in the car to redeem the time you spend waiting to pick up children from activities, in the doctor's office, and so on. My sons and I like to watch the Olympics, but there's a lot of down time during commercials and while waiting for events to start, so one summer I made a list of small tasks that didn't require a lot of focused thought that I could do during those times. Working on these allowed me to prepare for our new school year, plan an upcoming trip, and spend more time watching the actual events with my boys. Perhaps this list will spark your own creative ideas for ways you can multitask effectively:

- sew on Scout badges

- update bill payment list

- catalog new books

- complete insurance paperwork

- check in shipment of books for homeschool co-op

- prepare school binders with dividers

- compile syllabus for literature class

- learn to use my new phone

- type book shopping list

- type Colorado contacts and itinerary

- file paperwork

We'll consider more ways to use small blocks of time effectively in chapter 4.

Use Your Tools Wisely

These tools are not sequential, but they all work together. Reflecting helps you identify your focus, and educating yourself opens your mind to possibilities. Eliminating and self-discipline help you maintain your focus. Organizing helps you eliminate, and multitasking frees up time to reflect and educate.

> Productivity is never an accident. It is always the result of a commitment to excellence, intelligent planning, and focused effort.
> PAUL J. MEYER

When you use these tools wisely, you won't be paralyzed by what you can't do. You'll begin to find peace in the space between the ideal and reality, and you'll enjoy a more productive, balanced life.

Take Action!

❏ How will you implement each of the FREEDOM tools for meeting all the obligations and challenges of your life?

- **F**ocus: What is it that only you *can* do? What is it that only you *should* do? How will you prioritize these things?

- **R**eflect: How will you set aside some quiet time alone to reflect?

- **E**ducate: Are you sharpening your skills and broadening your mind? How will you find a way to make learning a regular part of your life?

- **E**liminate: What activities do you need to stop? What opportunities do you need to say no to? What can you delegate? What can you outsource?

- **D**iscipline: How would you rate your level of self-discipline? Are you abusing your freedom and flexibility? Are you doing what you know you need to do? How can you improve in this area?

- **O**rganize: Is your life generally organized or disorganized? How can you do a better job of organizing your time, tasks, thoughts, and things?

- **M**ultitask: Is mental multitasking undermining your focus? If so, how will you change that habit? What are some ways you can multitask effectively by combining physical tasks with lighter mental tasks?

CHAPTER 4

Where Did My Time Go?

*Don't say you don't have enough time. You have exactly the same
number of hours per day that were given to Helen Keller, Pasteur,
Michelangelo, Mother Teresa, Leonardo Da Vinci, Thomas Jefferson,
and Albert Einstein.*
H. JACKSON BROWN, JR., *Life's Little Instruction Book*

Have you ever thought, "I could finally get everything done if I just
had more than twenty-four hours in a day?" I've certainly fantasized
about having more hours in my day! Time is our most priceless
resource because it's the one thing we can't get more of. Each of us
is allotted 168 hours a week—no more, no less.

Think of the most productive people you've ever met or heard
of—prolific authors, military commanders, political leaders, dedi-

cated missionaries, brilliant inventors, CEOs of high-profile companies, tireless volunteers, and so on. Now think of the *least* productive people you have ever met or heard of. They *all* have exactly the same amount of time each day. And so do you.

> All we have to decide is what to do with the time that is given us.
> J.R.R. TOLKIEN
> *The Fellowship of the Ring*

The difference is that some people use their time much more efficiently and effectively than others. Learning how to protect and prioritize your time will help you be a good steward of the time you've been given and use it for what's most important.

Keep a Time Log

How often do you reach the end of the day and wonder, "Where did the time go?" This exercise will help you answer that question definitively.

What's the first step when trying to improve your finances? Keep a meticulous record of how you spend every penny. Many wealthy people identify this approach as key to their financial success. Dieters often keep a food diary of everything they eat to make them more aware of calories and nutrition. The same technique works for improving your use of time. Until you know exactly where your time is going, you can't make wise decisions about how to allocate it better. Facing the reality in black and white will make you more conscious of your choices, whether it's how you're spending money, choosing what to eat, or using your time.

This may be the most important exercise in this book. It's also the one you're most likely to want to skip. Don't. You may think you have a pretty good idea of how you're using your time, but most people's estimates of their time expenditures differ wildly from their actual documented usage by the clock. Doing this exercise is necessary for you to gain the most value from the practical strategies I'll be sharing in the coming chapters.

Here's your assignment: Keep a record of how you spend your time every day, in half-hour increments, for at least a week. Choose a fairly typical week (not a vacation or holiday) and start as soon as possible. If your schedule varies a lot from week to week, you might want to track more than one week. But for most people, a one-week sample is enough.

You can keep your time log in a simple spiral notebook, or you can use the form provided in appendix B. This exercise may seem tedious at first, but it's important to stay as current as you can. Fill it out at least once every hour. It's too hard to remember what you did if you wait several hours or, worse, try to fill in the blanks at the end of the day. Don't worry about categorizing activities as you document them—you'll do that later when you assess your completed time log.

What kinds of activities should you record? Whatever you're doing! Cooking, cleaning, caring for a baby, showering, having a quiet time, homeschooling, planning lessons, taking your children on a field trip, doing laundry, keeping appointments, answering e-mail, practicing hobbies, running errands, reading, spending time with friends, working on business projects, going to church, paying bills, using social media, going on a date with your husband, playing a game as a family—everything.

Continue reading in this book as you're keeping your time log. At the end of the week, evaluate your log with the instructions in the next section and use what you learn to help you begin making better decisions about the use of your time.

I work at home with my homeschooling family, and we're building several businesses to replace our current stream of income. By keeping track of my time and evaluating what I do each day, I was able to identify roadblocks that were preventing us from moving forward. I soon realized I was putting way too much on my plate each day, and by the end of the day I was so frustrated, I felt like a failure. It hurt to realize I couldn't do it all, but at the same time I have a lot more peace—and I have a measurable way to see if I'm truly progressing. My family says "Amen" because Mom is staying calm.

COLEEN MERK, Texas

Assess Your Time Log

At the end of the week, assess your time log. Identify the various tasks and activities on which you spent your time, and calculate how many hours you devoted to each task or category of tasks during the course of the week. Once you have the numbers, evaluate the results in the following ways:

1. Do a *reality check*. How do the numbers compare to how you tend to think you spend your time? If you're spending more time on certain tasks than you realized, can you work more efficiently? Or is this simply a reality to accept?

2. Look for *gaps*: What things that you should be doing or want to do are not reflected in how you spend your time?

3. Look for things that are *expendable*. What tasks or activities could you eliminate or delegate?

4. Look for *opportunities*. Are there little windows of time you could be using more effectively than you're currently doing?

Use an Ongoing Time Log

After you finish and assess your initial time log, you may want to continue tracking your time on a modified basis. I'm not suggesting that you log every half hour for the rest of your life. However, I have found that if I jot down my major activities in my planner each day, this keeps me from getting to the end of the day and saying, "Where did the day go? What did I get done?" When I write it down, I have a record.

This is particularly helpful if you have a home business, whether or not you are paid by the hour. It's distressingly easy to stay busy with work-related activities that seem productive but aren't actually producing any income. We'll talk more about this in chapter 15.

If you reach a new stage in your life when you start to feel overwhelmed again and you wonder where your time is going, keep the full-scale time log again for a week to reevaluate. As your children grow older, your life circumstances change, and your health changes, you will need to adjust your priorities and reconsider how you use your time.

Calculate the Opportunity Cost of Each Choice

It's critical that you place a high value on your time. Although interruptions can consume your time if you let them, you can be your own worst enemy when you devalue your time. Don't fritter the day away. Don't use your time lightly. You can't get any of it back.

Whether you realize it or not, you're prioritizing with every decision you make. It's uncomfortable to think about your time in those terms if you often find yourself getting bogged down with things you wouldn't normally identify as high priorities. So why not be more intentional about it? Choosing to do one thing with this moment in time (or this day or this week) means choosing not to do all the other things you could do with the same time.

Here's just one example. Homeschoolers are typically frugal, especially in one-income families. Frugality is wise, but it's also important to calculate the hidden cost of saving money. If you drive all over town to several different stores to save money on groceries, be sure to factor in the cost of gas and the wear and tear on your vehicle. If you spend $20 less on groceries but burn an additional $5 worth of gas, your total savings equal $15, not $20.

> Teach us to number our days aright, that we may gain a heart of wisdom.
> PSALM 90:12 (NIV)

You also need to consider the value of your time. The equation becomes even more complicated if you have a home business. When my business was just getting started, I used to spend a lot of time shopping at yard sales, looking for inexpensive clothing for my children. Eventually I realized that instead of spending four Saturday mornings hoping to randomly stumble across a suitable pair of jeans at a yard sale, I could recapture a lot of billable work time if I would just go directly to a department store where I knew I could find the styles and sizes I needed for my hard-to-fit son. For example, I could pay $5 for a pair of yard-sale jeans, or I could pay $30 for jeans at the store and still have enough time to earn $100 working at my business. If I choose to go the yard-sale route but don't factor in the value of my time, I might think I've saved $25 on jeans when the truth is I lost $75 in income. I have nothing against yard sales; they can be fun and even productive. This is just one example of the trade-off involved in choosing how to spend your time.

Develop the habit of asking yourself, "What am I saying no to when I say yes to this choice? Are there any hidden costs?" These questions will help clarify your thinking when making such decisions.

Establish a Schedule or Routine

There are two kinds of people: those who thrive on schedules and those who hate them. Regardless of which group you're encamped with, you still have to make intentional choices about how you use your time. The difference lies in how far in advance you make those choices.

A daily schedule with designated time slots for specific activities works well for some people. One homeschool mom showed me her personal spreadsheet schedule with a different color column for each family member. It is quite impressive, and it works for her family.

If I had to make—much less follow—a time-specific schedule for the five people in my family, I would break out in hives. It works better for me to think in terms of a routine, not a schedule. The difference between routine and schedule is that with a schedule, specific things are meant to happen at specific times. With a routine, specific things happen in a specific order. We get up in the morning and do our morning routine—breakfast, shower, chores, etc.—and then we have school time, then lunch, then work, and so on.

Our homeschool time isn't divided into science at 9:00, math at 10:00, and so on, because it can be hard to predict how long a particular lesson may take. I believe it's more productive (and less stressful) to give yourself and your kids the freedom to finish an assignment or project before moving on to the next one, rather than shifting gears when a bell or timer goes off like it would in an institutional school setting. Yes, it's important that your children learn how to be on time. However, going to church, field trips, meetings, homeschool co-ops, sports practice, music lessons, and other time-specific events provides plenty of opportunity to build a habit of punctuality. Following a routine rather than a schedule for lessons isn't an excuse for dawdling. As long as my boys get their assignments done during the course of the week, it doesn't matter much how they divide them up, and they learn to take responsibility for their own use of time. I'll talk more about this in chapter 13.

> Really creative, innovative thinking seems to come out of chaos more often than out of neatnik organization, but the successful implementation of innovative ideas seems to come about in a most organized, disciplined way.
> DAN KENNEDY
> Entrepreneur

If a schedule with time slots works well for you, keep using it. If you have always resisted schedules or they don't work well for you, see if you can figure out why. If it's simply because you're undisciplined, you may need to experiment with a schedule to develop more accountability. If it's truly not a good fit for you and your family, perhaps because you have a more creative temperament, think in terms of a routine rather than a schedule.

There's no one right way to schedule your day, so don't let anybody make you feel guilty for doing what works best for your family. Flexibility is an essential part of finding balance on a daily basis. We'll talk about handling interruptions to your schedule or routine in chapter 7. Meanwhile, keep that tightrope walker in mind and practice the habit of making small, frequent adjustments as needed to keep your life balanced.

Use Small Blocks of Time Wisely

Learn to capture even brief opportunities to accomplish small tasks or small portions of bigger tasks. There are lots of things you can get done in five-, ten-, or fifteen-minute intervals.

For example, I recently had about fifteen minutes before I had to leave for an appointment, and I decided that was exactly the amount of time I needed to take care of something that had been driving me crazy every morning. My bathroom counter was so cluttered that there wasn't a place for my hairdryer. All I needed to do was to sit on the floor and clear out all the stuff in the cabinets under the sink, throw away the junk that had accumulated, and organize the rest. In just fifteen minutes, I made space for my hairdryer in the cabinet, and the counter was clean and neat.

> Is not a day divided into twenty-four hours, each hour into sixty minutes, and every minute subdivided into sixty seconds? Now in 86,400 seconds very many things can be done.
> VICTOR HUGO
> *The Count of Monte Cristo*

This is a habit I have tried to teach my children. When they were younger, they were often frantically getting ready and running late when we needed to leave the house. Now that they're older, they're likely to be ready on time or even ahead of time, and they often just hang around aimlessly during for the last ten minutes before we go. I encourage them to use these waiting times to complete short tasks like folding and putting away a load of laundry, emptying the dishwasher, feeding the cats, or organizing their school papers. We're still working on developing this habit, but they're learning that using those brief opportunities to accomplish something will free up time later to do something they enjoy.

As we saw in the previous chapter, using small blocks of time is also a good way to multitask. If I'm talking on the phone, unless it's for business or serious conversation, I'll usually look for a small mindless task to accomplish while I talk, even if it's just walking around the yard to stretch my legs a bit.

What Can You Accomplish in 5–15 Minutes?

I surveyed moms for their best tips for using small blocks of time efficiently. Here are some of their suggestions.

- Wipe down kitchen counters and appliances. Clean out the refrigerator or freezer. Load or empty the dishwasher.

- Dust, sweep, mop, or vacuum one room. Dust the blinds on one window. Clean fingerprints off light switches and stair railings. Sweep the front porch.

- Wipe down a bathroom. Clean the toilet. Empty bathroom wastebaskets.

- Straighten a drawer. Clear off the desk. Pick up the clutter in one room. Make beds. Organize a bookshelf.

- Change batteries in the smoke detectors. Water the houseplants. Sort old magazines and newspapers for recycling.

- Fold or hang up a load of laundry. Sort and distribute clean clothes to their owners for folding.

- Make the menus for the week. Inventory the pantry. Write the shopping list. Put a meal together in a slow cooker. Wash and prepare the week's fruits and vegetables.

- Break fallen branches into kindling and build a fire in the woodstove.

- Pay a few bills. Renew library books online. Schedule a doctor, dentist, salon, or vet appointment.

- Write a note of thanks, condolence, "get well," etc. Encourage a friend on Facebook and say a prayer for her.

- Write lesson plans for one child or one subject.

- Read a picture book to your kids. Tell them a story from your childhood. Tickle a toddler.

Take Advantage of Unexpected Opportunities

Sometimes you're presented with slightly longer opportunities to do something productive. My webmaster and I planned the website for the "How Do You Do It All?" class during a half-hour break before supper at a conference we both attended. We were chatting casually about what I wanted to do with the website and realized we could get started right away. We pulled out our laptops, sat down side by side, and worked out all the pieces we needed to get in place, including sales copy, a shopping cart, autoresponder, and so on. We took advantage of that half-hour, and we got it done.

Sometimes there are even longer blocks of time. One of my students thought my class was on Tuesday night, so she set aside that time. When she realized the class was actually scheduled for Thursday, I asked her, "What are you going to do with this hour and a half you've set aside?" I wanted to point out that it was a gift to have that blocked-off time suddenly available for her use.

Something similar happened to me on a larger scale several years ago. I was invited to speak at a business conference along with some really high-profile speakers, and I was thrilled about the opportunity. I scheduled an entire month when I didn't accept any other business projects so I could spend that whole month preparing for the event. Unfortunately, the conference was cancelled about a month before it was to take place. I was so disappointed, but instead of whining about it—remember the no-whining rule!—I suddenly realized that if I looked at it another way, I had just been given the gift of a month of available work time.

That's when I finally developed my class on how to start a home-based business as a freelance editor. I had been thinking about this for two years but had never made time for it. I took that unexpected opportunity—a block of time that had suddenly been freed—and developed a course that I continue to sell today.

Do What You Can

Sometimes it's easy to become paralyzed by an overwhelming list of things to do. It's tempting to think, consciously or unconsciously, "I can't do it all, so I'm just not going to do anything." If you recognize this tendency in yourself, nip it in the bud. Or maybe you're waiting for "someday" down the road to do what matters most. Resolve instead

> Do what you can, with what you have, where you are.
> THEODORE ROOSEVELT

to be a good steward of your time *now*. Do what you can, in the situation you're in, with the time that you have. Over the course of time, "what you can" will expand, and you'll come closer to doing "it all."

Take Action!

❒ Keep a time log—a record of how you spend your time every day, in half-hour increments—for at least a week. (There's a form in appendix B.) Continue reading in this book while you're keeping your log. At the end of the week, assess your time log. Identify the activities on which you spent your time, sort them into categories (such as sleep, exercise, personal hygiene, housekeeping, cooking, errands, church, homeschooling, family time, hobbies, business activities, etc.) and calculate how many hours you spent on each category of activities. Then evaluate your results in the following ways:

1. Do a *reality check*. How do the numbers compare to how you tend to think you spend your time? If you're spending more time on certain tasks than you realized, can you work more efficiently? Or is this simply a reality to accept?

2. Look for *gaps*. What things that you should be doing or want to do are not reflected in how you spend your time?

3. Look for things that are *expendable*. What tasks or activities could you eliminate or delegate?

4. Look for *opportunities*. Are there little windows of time you could be using more effectively than you're currently doing?

❏ Would using some kind of time log on an ongoing basis be useful for you? Try using a less detailed log for a week and see whether it helps.

❏ As you make decisions about how to use your time, re-member to calculate the opportunity cost of each choice. Ask yourself, "What I am saying no to when I say yes to this choice? Are there any hidden costs?"

❏ Does a schedule or a routine work better for your family? Why? Do you need to make any changes in this area?

❏ Make a list of ways you can use small blocks of time wisely. Keep it handy and consult it whenever you have 5–15 minutes to do something productive.

❏ Don't become overwhelmed by your to-do list. Resolve to be a good steward of your time *now* rather than wait-ing for "someday" to do what matters most. Commit to doing what you can, in the situation you're in, with the time that you have.

CHAPTER 5

Aim High: Setting Goals

*He who every morning plans the transactions of the day, and
follows out the plan, carries on a thread which will guide him through
the labyrinth of the most busy life. . . . But where no plan is laid, where
the disposal of time is surrendered merely to the chance of incidents, all
things lie huddled together in one chaos.*
Hugh Blair, Scottish minister

A few months before his thirteenth birthday, my oldest son, Forrest,
wrote down 101 goals for his life because he had heard Mark Victor
Hansen, coauthor of the *Chicken Soup for the Soul* series, suggest it at
a business conference we'd attended. Forrest's goals included some
silly things like eating forty chocolate bars or drinking fifty soft
drinks in a row, but they also included some serious things and some

really big dreams for his life. In fact, it would take more than one lifetime to accomplish everything on his list!

Within seven months of writing down his 101 goals, this is what Forrest accomplished: He studied tornadoes and saw one live, learned about investing in the stock market, met Prince Edward of England, won a new Dell computer, did missions work here in Mississippi, learned about Internet marketing, launched his first website, gained experience in public speaking, took his first airplane flight, and traveled to Peru to help a missionary friend. If my thirteen-year-old kid could meet all these goals—some of them pretty big—in a little over half a year, I can think a little bigger and stretch a little farther too.

Any discussion of setting goals triggers an interesting variety of reactions. Some people nod in agreement that this is a useful, necessary thing. Some may even think, "I've already got this goal-setting thing down pat, so I don't need to learn anymore." Others groan, "Oh, I don't want to set goals. It's never worked for me." But it's absolutely essential that you set goals. It's one of the most important things you can do if you hope to achieve anything worthwhile. As Zig Ziglar was fond of saying, "If you aim at nothing, you will hit it every time."

Whether goal-setting is old hat or terra incognita, this chapter is for you.

I guess I do have a home-based business—homeschooling! I save thousands of dollars a year for my family by schooling at home instead of a Christian private school. After separating my goals, it helps me to see that not all my goals are about me. Many are for my family and homeschool.
KRISTEN JOHNSON, Arizona

Set Goals in Three Major Categories

When setting short- or long-term life goals, I have found it extremely helpful to think in terms of three categories:

- personal

- family

- business

When you homeschool and/or have a home business, there's some overlap among these categories, but everything you do will fit into at least one of them. If you don't have a home business, you may even want to think of homeschooling as your business.

We'll explore these categories in more detail in chapter 6 when we consider the seven planning tools. Some of the tools also include categories for service and reading, but even those fit within the big three. For example, a volunteer activity such as visiting a nursing home is something you can do (1) as an individual, (2) with your family (possibly as part of a homeschool group or church), or (3) as an outreach from your business. Reading can be (1) for personal entertainment, enrichment, or education, (2) for your homeschool or to enhance your homemaking skills or family life, or (3) to help you grow your business.

Make Your Goals Specific and Measurable

Goals should be specific and measurable, not vague and general like "Be more patient with my children" or "Get more done." If you can't measure it, how can you know if you did it?

For example, instead of setting a goal to get more exercise, a specific goal could be to walk at least thirty minutes, at least five days a week. That's easy to measure. Did you walk thirty minutes? And did you do it five days? Yes or no—very clear-cut.

If your goal is to do more fun things as a family, choose a specific activity, like spending an hour reading aloud one night this week, playing a board game for family night, or having a picnic at the park on Saturday. You need to be able to look back at the end of the week and either say yes, you did it, or no, you didn't.

Think Big

Kids instinctively think big. When Andrew was eleven, he often photocopied editing projects for me. One day he said, "Maybe I can get a job doing this for other people." "You probably could," I replied, "but you'd only make minimum wage." He responded in disbelief, "Minimum? Why can't I have the maximum one?" He had a lot to learn about economics and relative pay scales, but I loved his automatic inclination toward the maximum.

As we grow older, however, the everyday demands of life often crowd big thinking from our minds. If you're in the early years of having babies and training toddlers, just getting a decent night's sleep can seem like an unattainable aspiration. Bringing up children well and creating a loving, vibrant home are important jobs with real eternal significance. Don't lose sight of

> Far better it is to dare mighty things, to win glorious triumphs, even though checkered by failure, than to take rank with those poor spirits who neither enjoy much nor suffer much, because they live in the gray twilight that knows not victory nor defeat.
> THEODORE ROOSEVELT

this on the inevitable hard days. Thinking big will look different at different stages of your life.

Charlotte Mason offers this wise counsel: "Do not let the endless succession of small things crowd great ideals out of sight and out of mind."[1] The Big Dream exercise in chapter 6 will help you open your mind to the possibilities. Live large, not small. Don't just settle for what's comfortable, but stretch yourself and grow.

Throughout this book, you'll find reminders to be realistic and to set manageable goals. Is it a contradiction, then, for me to urge you to think big? Absolutely not. The challenge is finding the right balance between setting realistic goals that you're likely to accomplish and stretching yourself by thinking big. One key is to set big long-term goals and smaller short-term goals. The seven planning tools in the next chapter will help you do just that.

Write Down Your Goals

It's important to commit your goals to writing. Unwritten goals are just talk. If you don't write them down, you'll tend to think in broader, vaguer terms, and you're much less likely to take action. When you write out your goals, they become more real, and you become accountable, even if it's just to that piece of paper.

> Thoughts tend to disentangle themselves when they flow over the tip of a pencil.
> DAWSON TROTMAN
> Founder of the Navigators

I used to have a personal goal to walk thirty minutes a day. One night I got a late start, my legs were sore, and I was ready to quit after only twenty minutes. Then I thought of that piece of paper with my goals and realized, "If I stop now, I can't check that off my list, and I'm going to be shortchanging myself." Because I had written down my goal, I kept walking for ten more minutes. My legs didn't hurt any worse, and I had the satisfaction of knowing I had met the goal I'd set for myself.

A big key to success for me is that the more I write down, the less I have in my brain. The less I have swirling around in my brain, the better I can focus on the task at hand without having to worry about what is next or if I'm forgetting anything. And I'm actually less irritable with my children.
MOM IN THE "HOW DO YOU DO IT ALL?" CLASS

When you start using the seven planning tools, you may be surprised at first how hard it is to decide what goals to set, especially on your Weekly Plan. When you don't write things down, you can fool yourself much more easily ("I've got three million things to do this week, but I can do them!"). But when you write your three million items on a list where you can see them and you think of those twenty-four hours in a day, you quickly realize you're going to have to make some tough choices. You may be dismayed or even overwhelmed by the wide gap between what you need to do and the amount of time available when you see it starkly in black and white (or even in color).

Writing it all down forces you to be intentional—not to choose on a whim but to plan, prioritize, and make sure the important things are getting done, even if not *everything* is getting done. Remember my answer to the question "How do you do it all?" I don't, and I redefine "it all." *Nobody* can do it all. We all have to make tough choices when it comes to setting priorities. Writing things down will help you do that wisely.

I am so much more fruitful and focused when I keep written goals. There is magic in the mind-body connection when I pen them with my own hand. Even in rereading them, my handwriting evokes ownership of my goals, and that helps me to keep going and to fiercely defend my time and energies so that I can keep them.
HOLLY NELSON, Kansas

Share Your Goals

One good way for you to hold yourself accountable for meeting your goals is to share them with an accountability partner, coach, or mastermind team. In chapter 15, we'll look at the benefits of having a mastermind team or coach for your business, but even if you don't have a business, sharing your goals with a friend or accountability partner provides great incentive to stay on track.

I was struggling to be consistent in taking a lot of nutritional supplements that are very important for some health issues I'm dealing with. It's never been easy for me to swallow pills, and it was becoming too easy to neglect them when I didn't feel well. I finally asked my mastermind team to hold me accountable until I firmly established the daily habit. I posted a comment on our private Facebook group every day when I finished taking all the supplements. I knew that if I didn't post, my teammates would ask about it. There were quite a few days when the *only* thing that made me swallow all those pills was knowing I'd have to face their questions!

Remember the business contest I mentioned in the introduction? At the time, I was working on editing projects for marketer Martin Wales and copywriter David Garfinkel, so I told both of them that my goal for the next year was to double my income and win the contest. I knew that they were rooting for me and that they believed in me. When I won the contest, it was such a delight to write to David and Martin and tell them about it. They both wrote back and said, "I knew you could do it." That was a tremendous encouragement.

Just like writing down your goals, sharing them really makes them come to life. Be sure to share only with people who will be encouraging and supportive as you strive to meet your goals.

Take Action!

☐ Have you already established the habit of setting goals? Why or why not? If not, consider how setting goals would help you and make a commitment to do it.

☐ Do you think big? Why or why not? Resolve to stretch yourself and get out of your comfort zone as you work through the remainder of this book.

☐ How will you hold yourself accountable for reaching your goals? With whom will you share your goals?

CHAPTER 6

What Do I Do Next?
Seven Essential Planning Tools

*These tools have given me a whole new mindset and have helped me
to live more proactively. Before, I had good intentions and good plans,
but they would often be derailed by life. I feel more in control now, and
I'm able to work out the nitty-gritty details much more easily. I'm no
longer as apt to drop the ball of planning ahead and working my plan.*
JOY CONSTANT, mom from Louisiana

Everyone needs both short-term and long-term goals. Your long-
term vision and yearly goals should drive your weekly plans and
daily tasks. When we build our lives around short-term tasks, we
tend to live in triage mode, focusing on the urgent to the neglect

of the important.

I have found these seven planning tools to be essential:

1. Big Dream

2. Yearly Goals

3. Monthly Calendar

4. Weekly Plan

5. Daily Tasks

6. Running To-Do List

7. Stop-Doing List

The order of this list is important, although you may not necessarily create them in this order. The "Where Do You Start?" section at the end of this chapter will help you decide how to begin.

Samples of these forms are provided in appendix B, and you can download customizable versions free at www.FlourishAtHome.com/book. If you already have a favorite planner or app, you can use it to implement the principles in this book, whether your planner is paper or digital, simple or elaborate, schedule grids or open-ended forms. No planner will work well unless you have a system for deciding what to write in it. This book is not primarily about what boxes to put things in, but about figuring out what things to put in the boxes.

If seven planning tools seem a bit overwhelming, feel free to tweak them to fit your situation. Just keep in mind that no matter how many forms or lists you use, you still have to make decisions in each of these seven categories.

1. Big Dream

The first and most important part of planning is establishing a long-term vision. This made a huge difference in my life. In 2004, a dear friend, Louise Jones of California, challenged my first mastermind team to answer three important questions:

1. What would I be doing if nothing stood in my way?

2. What stands in my way?

3. What do I need to do to achieve my goals?

I call the answers to these three questions the "Big Dream." I keep mine in my purse so it's with me everywhere I go. Remember that trip to the Grand Canyon? It was on my Big Dream list!

Set aside some time to start thinking about your own answers to these questions. (See the Big Dream form in appendix B.) Write down your answers, and then put them in your binder (and your purse!). Write down everything that comes to mind to answer question 1, even if you have no idea how you might accomplish it. The point of this exercise is to expand the scope of your thinking, remove the limitations, and imagine all the possibilities.

> Thinking big creates the excitement necessary for accomplishment.
> ZIG ZIGLAR

This is a great way to learn to think big. Focus will come later as you decide what to do. Obviously, you can't do all those Big Dream things at once. If you can, you're not dreaming big enough. One mom told me, "I found that my big dreams were not very big at first, and then I ended up putting down so many things. I thought I dreamed big, but I realized that I was initially only looking past the current situation our family is in right now."

Here's just one example from my own Big Dream. When I first did this exercise, one of my answers to question 1 was this: "I would offer encouragement, hope, and assistance to others, beginning in my local church and including single mothers, especially single mothers whose desire is to remain at home with their children." I was delighted to give several single homeschooling moms free access to my original "How Do You Do It All?" class. I also started a blog at www.SingleParentsAtHome.com, and I've been blessed with many opportunities to speak and write about single-parent homeschooling that I could never have imagined when I first wrote that goal.

Jan Karon—my favorite author—is an inspiring example of someone who had the courage to pursue her dream. She had longed to be a writer from age ten, when she wrote her first novel. At age fifty, she left a lucrative career in advertising and moved to a little mountain village to focus on writing fiction. The first few years were challenging, and she supported herself through a recession with freelance copywriting while she wrote *At Home in Mitford*. Her delightful novels have become bestsellers, won awards, and blessed millions of readers around the world. In an interview with CBN, Jan offered this advice: "If God has given you a dream, you'd better get cracking because He wants to use it."[1]

2. Yearly Goals

The second tool is your list of Yearly Goals. These goals should be in alignment with your Big Dream. If they aren't, there's a disconnect and that's a problem. If you find that your Yearly Goals and Big Dream are not aligned, reevaluate both to determine what you really want.

If possible, set aside the last week of every year for review, planning, and goal setting. Take out your calendar now and block out December 26–31 for planning and setting goals. Can't take a whole week for that? Take a weekend. If you can't take a weekend, take a day. But set aside a significant block of time to think, dream, plan, and evaluate.

First you'll look back, and then you'll plan ahead. Look back over the entire year. Review your personal, family, and business activities and accomplishments and assess how well they matched your goals. Then set new goals for the coming year, keeping in mind your long-term vision, or Big Dream.

Later in this chapter, you'll learn how to create a Weekly Plan that also serves as a record of your accomplishments. Reading through your Weekly Plan is a great way to begin your yearly review. The main difference between your weekly and yearly lists is that the Weekly Plan is chronological and more detailed, while the Yearly Goals and assessment are more topical. If you don't have a weekly goals record for this year, just review your calendar and any other records you've kept.

> Be at war with your vices, at peace with your neighbors, and let every new year find you a better man.
> BENJAMIN FRANKLIN

Use the Yearly Review form in appendix B to evaluate your year in the following five categories:

- **Personal.** Include things like exercise, spiritual growth, hobbies, and things you do just for fun (not including family activities).

- **Family.** Include homeschooling and family activities such as field trips and travel, as well as a subcategory for each child's major accomplishments and activities. You may want to include activities with your extended family as well.

- **Business** (if applicable). Summarize your business activities for the year. The details will vary depending on your business, but you might include categories like sales figures, clients served, projects completed, products created, speaking engagements, and conferences attended.

- **Service**. How have you given back? Have you served in your church, volunteered at a food bank, counseled a hurting friend?

- **Reading**. I cut and paste this from my ongoing list of books I've read. (I've been tracking my reading since 1986.) This might be overkill for some folks, but I like to see everything for the year in one place. Tracking your reading provides a gauge of your interests, your focus, and how you're growing.

After completing the yearly review, compare it to your goals for the year to see how well you've stayed on track. What goals did you reach? What fell through the cracks? Did your priorities change during the year? If you didn't write goals for the past year, just assess how productive your year was and use the information to help set a direction for the following year.

If there's not a lot of correlation between what you planned and what actually happened, you need to ask yourself some questions: Was the problem in the planning or the execution? Was there a life crisis, one of those irreducible facts that intervened? Be honest with yourself so that you can achieve a closer alignment between your goals and reality the next year.

Now that you've looked back, you're ready to look ahead.

1. Review your Big Dream. Has it changed? Do you need to add or subtract items? Use this long-term vision to help set your Yearly Goals.

2. Use the Yearly Goals form in appendix B to write down specific, measurable goals for the coming year in the three major categories—personal, family, and business. You can integrate service and reading goals here or place them in separate sections. Aim for a balance between realistic and ambitious. Your goals should be doable, but they should also stretch you.

3. Mark your Monthly Calendar for the year with birthdays, holidays, and any other date-specific events you have already planned, such as vacations or conferences. Remember to schedule time between Christmas and New Year's Day for your next yearly review and goal planning.

As you evaluate the year that's ending and plan the year ahead, always keep your Big Dream in mind.

3. Monthly Calendar

The third level of planning is your Monthly Calendar. The activities you mark on it should be in line with your Yearly Goals.

Appendix B includes a calendar so you can see an entire month at a glance. Post the current month's calendar where you'll see it daily, and store the other months in your binder.

Your calendar of monthly priorities should include everything that is date-specific, such as holidays, medical appointments, vacations, children's sporting events, meetings with clients, etc. (You will already have filled in things like holidays and birthdays during your yearly planning.) Those little box-es aren't big enough to make a full itemized list for each day, so just hit the high points. Your Weekly Plan and Daily Tasks lists will be more detailed.

> We must not allow the clock and the calendar to blind us to the fact that each moment of life is a miracle and mystery.
> H. G. WELLS

I color-code my calendar be-cause otherwise everything becomes one big blur. Use different categories or add your own colors to suit your unique obligations. Or use all one color if this seems like overkill. Here's how I do it:

- Purple—celebrations such as birthdays and holidays

- Pink—personal commitments, such as Mom's Night Out or doctor appointments

- Gold (the gold standard for a quality education)—homeschool activities

- Blue—family activities that involve me

- Brown—my sons' activities that don't involve me

- Green (the color of money)—business

- Red—unusual, urgent, or especially important commitments

- Black—anything else

I began using two colors (blue and brown) for family activities once my boys began driving. Their piano lessons and sports practices don't require my presence anymore, but I need to keep those activities in mind so I don't schedule other things, like dentist appointments, at the same time.

Schedule time to review your Yearly Goals on the first Sunday of each month to help you stay on track throughout the year. If you don't look back at your goals, you'll tend to lose your focus and accomplish much less of what you set out to do.

4. Weekly Plan

The Weekly Plan is the key to this system. We tend to think naturally in terms of weeks, and a week is the most strategic unit for good planning. A month is too long and a day is too short for the necessary combination of big picture and detail.

Record your goals for each week in the Weekly Plan in appendix B. Just as you do with your Yearly Goals, you'll look at each week twice: once looking ahead to plan, and once looking back to review and evaluate. The Weekly Plan includes the same categories as the Yearly Goals:

- Personal

- Family

- Business

- Service

- Reading

Using these categories—especially the first three—helps you see the balance (or lack of it) in your life each week. You won't always have a perfect balance among the categories, and it's not just about the number of items in each group. Some weeks will necessarily lean more toward business, family, or personal commitments than others. But if you have twenty-five items in your business list, five in family, and zero in personal for several weeks in a row, you're headed for burnout fast!

I set goals in the personal, family, and business categories every week. Sometimes I set service goals, but more often that section serves as a record of the opportunities God has placed in my path, such as counseling and encouraging a single mom by phone. I always have several books in progress, so I use the reading section strictly as a log. If you're not already a regular reader, you'll need to set a specific goal in this category.

> Monday was the diving board poised over the rest of the week. One walked out on the board, reviewed the situation, planned one's strategy, bounced a few times to get the feel of things, and then made a clean dive. Without Monday, one simply bombed into the water, belly first, and hoped for the best.
> JAN KARON
> *At Home in Mitford*

Just half an hour of weekly planning will multiply your productivity and relieve stress and frustration.

PLANNING YOUR WEEK

As you plan your week, be sure to include the important things, not just the urgent things. The list does not include every single thing you will do in the week—just the must-do's, the date-specific commitments, and your top priorities. Avoid the temptation to cram too many things into your week. Leave some margin to deal with the unexpected.

It isn't necessary to include established habits. For example, if you've already established the habit of exercising every day or drinking eight glasses of water or going to church, that doesn't have to go on there because it has become part of the fabric of your life. But when you are working on forming new habits, such items need to go on your list until they become solidified—probably for at least a month.

Don't try to establish too many new habits at one time. When I started using this system, I was so gung-ho on this idea of planning, setting goals, and changing all the things in my life that needed to be changed that I went way overboard. The personal section of my weekly list had goals for drinking more water, taking nutritional supplements, going to bed at a certain time, waking up at a certain time, being more consistent about daily devotions, and exercising. You just can't focus on building that many new habits at one time, no matter how important they are. Focus on one or at most two new habits at a time.

Your list should include "go fors" as well as goals. Goals are promises that you make to yourself, while "go fors" are things you'd like to accomplish that week but that you know are going to be a stretch. You want to strike a balance between being realistic—setting goals you're pretty sure you can accomplish—and stretching yourself a bit by thinking big. You don't want it to be so easy that it's no sweat to meet your goals. On the other hand, you don't want your goals to be so optimistic that every week when you evaluate whether you met your goals (more on that below), you're constantly writing, "No," "No," "No," "No." You want to see mostly yeses on there. If you're consistently failing to meet your goals, something is wrong with either your execution or your goals.

Post your Weekly Plan where you can see it and mark off goals as you accomplish them. I keep mine on the bathroom mirror next to my Monthly Calendar, so I can review them while brushing my teeth or washing my hands. You might find another place that suits you better, such as a bulletin board in your office or even the kitchen. One of my mastermind partners, who had a goal to spend more time with her husband, realized it would undermine the value if he saw a reminder posted on the bathroom mirror! Use discretion in choosing where to post your goals.

> I had begun dreading Sunday nights because they were followed by Monday morning, which I dreaded even more because I was always feeling behind the eight-ball. My to-do list looked overwhelming. By dividing it up into three separate categories, I was able to better portion out the work I needed to do for the week.
> DAWN CLARK, Indiana

EVALUATING YOUR WEEK

The key to this Weekly Plan is evaluating at the end of the week. For each goal, ask yourself, "Did I do it or didn't I do it?" This is not about excuses; it's just about whether or not you did what you said you were going to do. Write "yes" or "no" after each goal on your list. If you completed part of a goal (such as walking only four days instead of the five you planned), make a note of it to remind yourself that you didn't ignore the goal entirely. You'll see examples of such notes in italics in my sample weekly plan in this chapter. Add a note about any significant things you did that weren't on your list. Keep this record in your binder as an encouraging reminder of what you have accomplished. This will also be invaluable when it comes time to do your yearly review.

Remember that "educate" is one of the FREEDOM tools. Ask yourself at the end of the week: What have I learned this week? Have I learned something about training and educating my children? Have I learned something new about working at home? Have I expanded my mind? Have I read anything challenging? Have I tried a new strategy? Try to learn something new every week.

As you assess each week, look for patterns of things you keep putting off. If a particular task stays on your list week after week because you never get around to doing it, don't beat yourself up about it. Instead, ask yourself *why* you're not doing it. There are usually two possible explanations: (1) You could be avoiding it, you might be procrastinating, or maybe you're just being lazy. Frankly, sometimes that's why I don't get things done. If the problem is you, you need to change something and discipline yourself to get it done; or (2) Maybe it's the task itself. Perhaps it doesn't really have to be done, and you can simply eliminate it. If it's a task that has to be completed but you're not the right person to do it, you can delegate it or outsource it.

Do your best to meet your goals, but be flexible and open to God's leading each day. Remember, "The mind of man plans his way, but the Lord directs his steps" (Proverbs 16:9). One mom told me, "I get the greatest satisfaction from sensing that no matter what did or didn't get done on my list, I have followed God's plan for the day." That's a wonderful attitude. I may post that above my own to-do list.

BE CONSISTENT

Schedule about thirty minutes to review the previous week and plan the week ahead. The best time for me to make this evaluation is on Sunday afternoons, as I finalize our homeschool lesson plans for the upcoming week at the same time. You may prefer Saturday. It's best not to wait until Monday morning, or you'll start off your week already behind. Find the time that works best for you and stick with it.

Since I began using this system, there have been a few times when I haven't done this weekly evaluation and planning because I thought I was "too busy." What a mistake! I've learned through experience that time "saved" by not planning isn't really saved at all; it's squandered (and more than offset) by the resulting frustration and inefficiency. No matter what, never skip your weekly planning.

MY SAMPLE WEEKLY PLAN

To give you an idea of what this system looks like in practice, here's a sample of my Weekly Plan and evaluation from September 2007:

PERSONAL:

Walk at least 30 minutes at least 5 days. NO.
> *Sun. 30, Mon. 30+15+25, Tues. 30 + basketball 45, Wed. 90*

Water: 5 glasses per day. Go for: 6. NO.
> *Sun. 4, Mon. 6, Tues. 3, Wed. 5, Thurs. 5, Fri. 4, Sat. 5*

Supplements every day. YES
Additional: Lunch with Coopers

FAMILY:

Prepare for Thomas's birthday. Go for: Work on costumes for Perry.
Had parties for Thomas AND Perry. Perry changed mind about costumes.

Homeschool co-op: Teach *Rasselas* in literature class. Begin preparing for *The Iliad.* View DVD project samples. YES

Send certificates of enrollment. YES

Start math with Forrest, Andrew, Perry; work with Thomas on phonics. YES

Boys visit their dad. NO *(He rescheduled.)*

Additional: Forrest ran with Spartans homeschool cross-country team in New Albany and came in 5th in Varsity Boys 5K.

BUSINESS:

Minimum 25 hours business this week. Go for: 35 hours. YES.
> *28.5 hours total – Mon. 4, Tues. 3.5, Wed 3.5, Thurs. 6, Fri. 3.5, Sat. 8*

Follow up with Atlanta contacts. YES

Promote "How Do You Do It All?" class; announce audio availability. YES

Prepare Top 10 report for survey respondents. YES

Begin preparing outline for "How Do You Do It All?" class. YES

Contact Mauricio [my business coach]. YES
Finish [curriculum editing project] introduction. NO
Go for: Polish editing course transcripts. NO
Additional: Sent editing quotes to C and J. Sent C sample to
    editing assistant.

SERVICE:
Counsel [single mom]. YES

READING:
Finished *Rasselas* by Samuel Johnson
Began *Rite of Passage Parenting* by Walker Moore
Began *The Iliad* by Homer

In the personal category, I walked more than the equivalent of thirty minutes on five days (for a total of 150 minutes), but since I didn't walk at least thirty minutes on five separate days, I marked that down as a no. Part of the goal was to build the habit of walking at least five days a week.

My family category varies a good bit. Some weeks include more specific, date-oriented family goals than others. Two of my children have September birthdays, so I wanted to start thinking about birthday parties for them. Their dad rescheduled the visit originally planned for that weekend, so I ended up having both parties that week. You'll notice I don't list homeschooling in general because that's an already established habit. We homeschool every weekday. However, I wanted to make sure I focused on math with my three oldest children and made it a priority to work with my youngest child on phonics, so I listed those specific homeschooling goals.

In the business category, I exceeded my goal to work a minimum of twenty-five hours that week but fell short of my "go for" goal of thirty-five hours. Since I met the basic goal, this was a yes. I included my daily work hours to help me see how they balanced out over the course of a week. Because the boys' visit was rescheduled and I went ahead with their birthday parties, I didn't complete my last goal and "go for" in the business section. Sometimes unavoidable circumstances intervene during the course of a week to change your goals, and the balance among categories inevitably shifts. That's OK—you can redistribute the balance the following week.

In the service category, I spent about an hour and a half on the phone talking with a single-mom friend. I walked around my neighborhood while I talked on my mobile phone. Walking didn't distract me from our conversation; in fact, it helped me focus. I was able to counsel my friend and get some exercise at the same time. That's effective multitasking.

In the reading category, I finished one book for our homeschool co-op literature class and started another. I also began reading a parenting book. All my reading that week was family-oriented. Some weeks include reading fiction for pleasure or reading nonfiction on business-related topics.

5. Daily Tasks

The fifth planning tool is a list of Daily Tasks, which is based on your Weekly Plan. This is your most detailed list. It includes everything that is time-specific, as well as your other tasks for the day. For example, running errands wouldn't go on your weekly list, but it does go on your daily list. You might list homeschooling every day, or you might regard that as a habit and just list specific things you really want to prioritize. You can arrange your list by time, priority, category, tasks that require leaving the house, tasks that must be done at a specific time, or any other grouping that proves useful for you.

Keep your list where you can see it and mark off items as you complete them. I keep my Daily Tasks list on my desk next to my computer. Unlike the yearly, monthly, and weekly planning forms, you don't need to keep the Daily Tasks list as an ongoing record. It's simply a working document that can be thrown away when you're finished with it.

When you plan your week, that's a good time to make a preliminary task list for each day of your week. Be sure to review and update each day's list the night before so you can hit the ground running the next morning. The more you tend to procrastinate, the more you need to schedule your work for specific days or even specific times at the beginning of the week. If you prefer to be more flexible, you can choose each day's activities from your Weekly Plan, as long as you have the self-discipline to finish everything within that week.

If there's an item you didn't get to on the designated day, reschedule it for another day. If you keep rescheduling the same task over and over, then you need to reevaluate it. Do you really need to do it at all? Can you eliminate it or delegate it? Or are you simply procrastinating?

Some people may feel that the daily list overlaps the weekly list too much. I've experimented with working straight from my weekly list, but a daily list forces me to make more conscious, intentional choices about my time and to allocate my priorities more effectively. Find what works best for you and stick with it.

> How we spend our days is, of course, how we spend our lives.
> ANNIE DILLARD

The daily decisions about how you will use your time are where you really have to fight off the "tyranny of the urgent," as Charles Hummel calls it. You must resist the ongoing temptation to cave in to whatever is urgent and let the important things slide.

I've been experimenting with a couple of variations on the Daily Tasks list. After I make my weekly schedule, I transfer everything immediately to the daily list and color code it with the same colors

I use for my Monthly Calendar. In one version of the list, I assign every single item to a particular day. In another version, the left column has day-specific items, and the right column has everything else I need to do sometime that week. Both lists are more detailed than the Weekly Plan for that week; going to the bank and Walmart show up on the daily list but not the weekly one. Don't let these variations confuse you. This is just an example of how you can tweak my tools to suit your own needs. I've found that I prefer the flexibility of the second version, but if I start to get slack about what I need to do each day, the first version works better.

> Look at a day when you are supremely satisfied at the end. It's not a day when you lounge around doing nothing; it's when you've had everything to do, and you've done it.
> MARGARET THATCHER

On pages 80 and 81 you see two versions of my Daily Tasks from the week I sent the first draft of this book to my editor at Apologia. (You can see color-coded versions at www.FlourishAtHome.com/book.) To keep my lists as concise as possible, I use lots of initials and abbreviations, such as B, L, and S for breakfast, lunch, and supper and F, A, P, and T for my children's names.

So how did the week turn out?

I added two service opportunities in response to requests from friends. One friend's sons spent Thursday night with us so she and her husband could counsel another couple. I also phoned a dear friend who had recently lost her husband to cancer and needed encouragement about how she could adjust to being alone and continue to homeschool her children. These were both important, and I was thankful I had the flexibility to help both of them. I also

DAILY TASKS SAMPLE 1:
Everything Allocated to a Specific Day

SUN 10/21
10:30 — church
supplements: BLS

MON 10/22
4:00 — A: piano
4:30 — chiropractor
6:00 — Scouts: coupon books
8:00 — pres. debate; sew on Scout badges
walk
supplements: BLS
A: call Mr. Randy
call Salvation Army re: donating mattress
errands: bank deposit, groceries
order lunch for co-op
A: Colorado pics; load my iPod
P: clean fridge; weed
ACT essay prep with A
check schoolwork
send book draft to Zan
edit JB's book
contract & invoice to B

TUES 10/23
4:00 — P: Spartans XC
walk
supplements: BLS
schedule A's senior portrait
pay bills
study Dante
composition with T
essays with A
check schoolwork
finish editing JB's book
write book review for LB
edit BYG, ch. 7

WED 10/24
5:30 — church
walk

supplements: BLS
P: clean for PopPop
study Dante
composition with T
essays with A
check schoolwork
edit BYG, ch 8
begin editing BW course
send out surveys for book
send editing quote to TC

THURS 10/25
7:30 — take Dad to Summit
4:00 — P: Spartans XC
4:30 — chiropractor
6:00 — P & T: Ultimate Frisbee
Sarah's birthday
walk
supplements: BLS
Dante: read, type notes
composition with T
essays with A
check schoolwork
edit BYG, ch 9
edit BW course
begin revising my book

FRI 10/26
8:00–3:00 — A, P, T: Excelsior
1:00 — teach literature class: Dante
walk
supplements: BLS
edit BW course
work on my book

SAT 10/27
8:00 — A: ACT
8:00 — P: Boy Scout service project
supplements: BLS
work on my book

DAILY TASKS SAMPLE 2:
Date-Specific Tasks and Tasks for Entire Week

SUN 10/21
10:30 — church
supplements: BLS

MON 10/22
4:00 — A: piano
4:30 — chiropractor
6:00 — Scouts: coupon books
8:00 — pres. debate; sew on Scout badges
supplements: BLS
A: call Mr. Randy

TUES 10/23
4:00 — P: Spartans XC
supplements: BLS

WED. 10/24
5:30 — church
supplements: BLS

THURS 10/25
7:30 — take Dad to Summit
4:00 — P: Spartans XC
4:30 — chiropractor
6:00 — P & T: Ultimate Frisbee
Sarah's birthday
supplements: BLS

FRI 10/26
8:00–3:00 — A, P, T: Excelsior
1:00 — teach literature class: Dante
supplements: BLS

SAT 10/27
8:00 — A: ACT
8:00 — P: Boy Scout service project
supplements: BLS

PERSONAL:
walk at least 25 min., 4 days

FAMILY:
order lunch for co-op
call Salvation Army re: donating mattress
schedule A's senior portrait
errands: bank deposit, groceries
pay bills

BOYS:
A: CO pics; load my iPod
P: clean fridge; weed
P: clean for PopPop

HOMESCHOOL:
ACT essay prep with A daily
composition with T daily
check schoolwork daily
study Dante, type notes

BUSINESS:
send my book draft to Zan
send out surveys for my book
begin revising my book
finish editing JB's book
edit BYG, ch 7–9
send contract & invoice to B
begin editing BW course
send editing quote to TC
write book review for LB

invited my dad to join us for dinner on Tuesday before his trip to Gatlinburg. I read an Agatha Christie novel and listened to an audiobook while driving to errands and appointments.

I walked only three days instead of four because I injured my Achilles tendon while walking too fast on hills. (This eliminated my walking for exercise for several more weeks.) I multitasked by sewing on Boy Scout badges while watching the presidential debate with the boys. One of my boys also joined me for each walk. I spent time every day helping Andrew prepare for the essay portion of the ACT. I also started a new composition program with Thomas; we worked on it two of the four scheduled days. I added "check schoolwork" to the daily list because I wanted to rebuild the habit of checking the boys' work every day instead of letting it pile up, and this helped me stay on track. I sent my manuscript to my editor on Monday but did not spend any more time on my book during the rest of the week. I began editing the BW course two days later than planned, and I edited only two of the three scheduled chapters of BYG. I did not write the book review for LB. Everything else happened as scheduled.

That sounds like a *lot* of tweaking, doesn't it? But that's OK. My end-of-the-week assessment showed me that I had been overambitious about how much time would be available for business with the extra family commitments, but I accomplished all of my most important tasks and shifted the unfinished items to the following week. I was satisfied.

6. Running To-Do List

The sixth planning tool is a Running To-Do List. This is simply an all-purpose, temporary holding place for unloading your brain so it won't have to spin its wheels reminding you. Write down *everything* you need or want to remember—no matter how big or small, no matter whether it's short-term or long-term. You'll keep adding to it over time. Yes, it will be a big unwieldy list, but it's already an unwieldy mass in your brain, occupying space you need for operating—kind of like RAM in a computer. At some point you may want to group the items into categories, but don't bother with that in the beginning unless it comes naturally to you. The main thing is just to get it all written down.

> "I wrote them down in my diary so that I wouldn't *have* to remember."
> PROFESSOR HENRY JONES
> *Indiana Jones and the Last Crusade*

Keeping a single Running To-Do List is much more efficient than jotting notes on random scraps of paper. You won't have to wonder, "Now where did I write that down?"

Some small tasks can be handled immediately without ever being written down. Take care of little things that will take only a few minutes right away instead of writing them down—if you set them aside to do later, they'll become more of a burden. This might include tasks like sorting the mail, paying bills, or sending a get-well card to a friend. An important caution: Don't fall into the trap of letting little things eat up your time. Sometimes it's more efficient to create a group of related tasks to handle all at once—sorting the mail, paying bills, and sending a get-well card all fall in the category of correspondence, which you could assign a regularly scheduled time each week. Make sure you're not spending your time on a lot of minutiae and avoiding the big, important tasks.

Anything that can't be done right away needs to go on the Running To-Do List. Mine includes things like books I want to read, downloaded teleseminars I need to listen to, details about an upcoming Boy Scout campout, a preliminary Christmas shopping list, websites friends have recommended, upcoming editing jobs, and projects I'm considering. Some of these end up on various project-specific lists, but most things that don't have to be done right away stay parked here for a while.

I used to have one long overwhelming list. Finally I wised up and realized that the same categories I use for all my planning would work there too. I keep the top priorities for each category on the first page and divide the rest of the list into categories, with sub-lists for specific projects. Keeping the list on a computer makes it searchable. If you want to look for a specific piece of information, you can find it more easily on a computer document than on a lengthy handwritten list.

This list will work *only* if you review it periodically—preferably once a month. My Running To-Do List once reached eighteen pages before I got serious about evaluating it! If something stays on there too long, maybe you don't really need to do it after all.

7. Stop-Doing List

The seventh planning tool is a Stop-Doing List that balances and offsets the Running To-Do List. It's imperative to make decisions about what is and is not worth your time. This list helps you implement the "eliminate" strategy from the FREEDOM toolbox.

I first got the idea of a Stop-Doing List from *Good to Great* by Jim Collins, who conducted a five-year study of companies that made the transition from being good companies to being great companies. He found that companies which moved from good to great "did not focus principally on what to do to become great. They focused equally on what not to do and what to stop doing."[2]

Implementing a Stop-Doing List was one of the keys to growing my business. The year I doubled my income and won the business-growth contest, I cut out several of my least profitable business endeavors, including some things I really enjoyed but that were not the best use of my time. Eliminating less-important tasks freed my time and energy for more important work.

As you dream big and set goals for accomplishing new things, you'll find you simply must cut out some existing obligations and activities. Remember, every choice you make has a potential opportunity cost. Whenever you choose to do one thing, you are choosing not to do everything else. Edit your life to make space for what's really important. It's wonderfully freeing!

> The Stop-Doing List was the biggest aha for me! Until my fifth child, I always had room for "one more thing" if it needed to be done. Then I suddenly ran out of time to do everything I wanted to do, and I had to prioritize. The Stop-Doing List made room for the higher priorities.
> STEPHANIE BUCKWALTER, Virginia

Where to Keep Your Planning Tools

You can store these tools electronically or on paper or both. Set up a folder on your computer and name it "Planning." To bump it to the top of your alphabetical list of folders for easy access, you can name it "A1 Planning." In this folder you can store both the blank forms and your filled-out versions.

If you prefer printed forms, designate a three-ring binder to store them. If you're crafty, you might choose to decorate it. Make it as simple or as elaborate as you want. I tape my current Monthly Calendar and Weekly Plan to my bathroom mirror because that's like Grand Central Station—I know I'm going to be in and out of there, and I'll see it often. I keep my Daily Tasks and time log on my desk.

Adjust your storage system to suit your needs. If you're on the go a lot, you might like to keep everything in your binder and take it with you. Or you may prefer to keep all your lists on your mobile phone. If you're at home a lot, you might choose to keep current lists visible in your house as I do.

Where Do You Start?

> Organized people don't trust their memory—they trust their lists.
> EILEEN ROTH
> *Organizing for Dummies*

As you incorporate all seven planning tools into your life, your yearly, monthly, weekly, and daily goals should flow directly from your long-term vision. That's why I recommend you schedule two hours for the Big Dream exercise within the next week. Once you complete the initial exercise, you will continue to refine and expand your dream for the rest of your life.

Meanwhile, you have to decide what to do this week and what to do today. The Weekly Plan is where the rubber meets the road, so begin that right away. Don't wait for Sunday—go ahead and plan the rest of the week, starting with today. Then this weekend, begin to establish the habit of weekly review and planning at a regular time. Once you have your Weekly Plan, you can begin allocating daily tasks.

Within a week, you should have at least a preliminary Big Dream in writing. Then you can create a list of Yearly Goals for the remainder of the current year and begin building your Weekly Plan based on those goals.

After you've completed your Big Dream exercise and written goals for the current year (which focus on the big picture), create your Stop-Doing List and Running To-Do List (which focus more on the details).

Take Action!

Note: Planning forms for several of these activities are provided in appendix B. Remember, it will take some time to incorporate all seven tools into your life. If it seems overwhelming, start with the Weekly Plan and Big Dream and then gradually add the others.

❐ Set aside one to two hours this week to begin answering the three Big Dream questions:

1. What would I be doing if nothing stood in my way?

2. What stands in my way?

3. What do I need to do to achieve my goals?

❐ Take out your calendar and schedule time between Christmas and New Year's Day to plan and set goals for next year.

❐ Fill out your Monthly Calendar.

❐ Set aside an hour this weekend to create your Weekly Plan for next week in these areas:

- Personal
- Family
- Business (if applicable)
- Service (may use as goals or record)

- Reading (may use as goals or record)

At the end of the week, evaluate whether you met your goals.

❐ Each night, make a list of Daily Tasks for the following day. Resist the tyranny of the urgent as you go through each day.

❐ Begin keeping a Running To-Do List as a temporary storage place for everything you need or want to remember to do. Be sure to review it periodically—preferably every month.

❐ Create a Stop-Doing List. Look back over your answers to the "eliminate" section of the action steps in chapter 3 to spark your thinking.

❐ Create a place to store your planning tools, whether digital or paper.

CHAPTER 7

We Interrupt This Program . . .

*I feel like an outfielder in a baseball game constantly fielding
whatever's hit at me.*
KRISTEN JOHNSON, mom from Arizona

It's hard [phone rings] to get [dryer buzzes] anything done [baby cries] when you're constantly [mysterious crash from the kitchen] being interrupted [doorbell rings].

No matter how well we manage our time, our best efforts are often undermined by interruptions. Interruptions can come from strangers, acquaintances, business associates, friends, or family. They can involve bad or good news, illness, ordinary events, or enticing opportunities. Whatever the source, they distract us from what we have planned to do, hinder our productivity, and upset our balance. They can trigger bad attitudes and make us frustrated or irritable. Even more insidiously, they can confuse us about what is really important. Our families are our primary mission, but other things—even good things—can lure us away from taking care of them properly and tempt us to see our children as hindrances rather than blessings.

In this chapter, we'll explore how to stay on course despite distractions, how to balance accessibility with age-appropriate boundaries for our children, and how to recognize when an interruption signals an opportunity we should take.

The Perception of Moms at Home

When you spend most of your time at home, some people assume that you are available anytime. After all, how busy can you possibly be? Homeschooling and working from home are so different from our society's norms that many people don't take them seriously. They may call you or stop by your house although they would never call you or stop by if you worked in an office. They may just want to chat, or they may ask for your help—perhaps to babysit their children or let the washing machine repairman into their house.

It's important to show God's love by serving people, but you can't be available on demand for everyone all the time without neglecting your own family. Think through your choices carefully and operate from an intentional plan for serving others instead of just reacting to whatever people throw at you. It's essential to establish some boundaries, or your true priorities will be completely undermined. Remember, you have only twenty-four hours each day, and saying yes to one thing means saying no to everything else at the same time.

Phone Calls and Texting

What is your most common interruption? For many people, it's the telephone, and the ubiquity of mobile phones has only exacerbated the problem. There is something powerful about a ringing phone or text alert, and most of us instinctively respond like Pavlov's dogs. But you don't have to reply immediately to every text or answer the phone every time it rings. If you are in the middle of a phonics lesson with your six-year-old or you're spending some focused time on a project, just let it ring. What's going to happen if you don't answer the phone? Think about it. You don't answer the phone when you're in the shower, do you? Yet the world doesn't come crashing to an end.

Caller ID lets you make an informed decision about whether or not to answer a call. You can avoid telemarketing calls or getting sidetracked by a chatty friend when you need to focus on something else. If you see that it's your husband or a child away at college or a client you've been trying to reach, you can choose to answer. When you can't or won't answer the phone, an answering machine or voice mail can do the job for you. Then you can decide whether to return the call and when.

Call waiting is helpful when you're expecting an important call,

> The telephone call is a breaking-and-entering that we invite by having telephones in the first place. Someone unbidden barges in and for an instant or an hour usurps the ear and upsets the mind's prior arrangements.
> LANCE MORROW
> "Hoy! Hoy! Mushi-Mushi! Allo" in *Time*

such as a call back from a doctor's office. You can temporarily turn off call waiting if you don't want to hear that annoying beep in the background during an important conversation. My system allows me to hit *70 before I dial the number, and call waiting is turned off during that call only. You can also set voice mail to pick up call-waiting calls that you choose not to answer when you're in another conversation. On many calling plans, you can arrange to receive an e-mail notification when you have a voice-mail message.

You can reply to some phone messages with an e-mail instead of a phone call. That way you're in control of the timing—you reply at your convenience according to your priorities. When people respond to your reply with e-mail, they are likelier to stay brief and on topic than if you return their call. I once spent over an hour on the phone with the mother of a student in my homeschool co-op class. We could have handled the actual issue related to my class in ten minutes, but she explained every obligation of all of her other children in detail. I'm not uninterested in her children, but I needed to spend that time with my own. I should have done a better job of keeping the conversation focused on the issue at hand; replying to her phone message with e-mail would have been more efficient for both of us.

> Unapologetically and proactively restore a sense of control. Preempt disruptions in advance. Interruptions coming to us by way of technology require our permission—we own the technology; it does not own us. Turn it off. Or don't answer.
>
> RICHARD A. SWENSON, MD
> *In Search of Balance*

Running a home business makes setting telephone boundaries even more challenging. Some businesses are more phone-dependent than others, but you shouldn't have to constantly interrupt family time to take business calls. We'll look at strategies for handling calls from clients and customers in chapter 15.

Today, because you can take your cell phone anywhere, people expect you to be available 24/7. Don't be. And when you're in the company of others, don't ignore them while you text or talk on the phone. That's an all-too-common practice, but it's rude and disrespectful. It's sad to see families or friends gathered around a dinner table while everyone's attention is focused on their phones. It's better to ignore phones than people.

The phone should be your servant, not your master. Don't let it throw your life out of balance. Take charge of your phone and use it in accordance with your priorities for your family and the kind of life you want to lead.

E-mail and Social Media

The Internet is a wonderful tool, but it can be as much of a hindrance as phones. It all depends on how you handle it. Discipline yourself to use e-mail and social media wisely and intentionally. Otherwise, they can expand to eat up not only all of your available time but also a lot of your time that's not really available in the first place.

Try not going online first thing in the morning; it's not the best use of that prime time. I do check my e-mail every morning to see if there are important messages from clients that need my immediate attention, but I have to be careful not to get sucked into reading all the other messages as well. A "quick" look at Facebook can soak up an hour before I realize it.

I receive hundreds of e-mails each week, so I've developed several strategies for dealing with them. Create message rules to automatically sort incoming messages into folders for friends, newsletters, homeschool co-ops or support groups, Yahoo groups, projects, and clients. This cuts down on the number of messages to weed through in your general inbox and helps you prioritize which messages to read. Force important folders to the top of the alphabetical list by putting AAA or A1 at the beginning of the folder name. Create subfolders where appropriate. For example, my folder for a frequent editing client includes subfolders for every book I work on for her. Whenever possible, act on e-mails right away so you don't have to handle them twice. When there are action items you need to save till later, a folder named "Action Items" or "AAA Reply Soon" is a good place to store them.

The best way to manage your time online is to minimize the amount of incoming information. Be intentional when subscribing to newsletters or blog feeds, joining Facebook groups, and deciding who and what shows up in your newsfeed. Reassess these choices from time to time. I've been ruthlessly unsubscribing from all but the most helpful or encouraging subscriptions to declutter my inbox.

Technology has made it possible to stay in touch with friends and family and make new acquaintances from all over the world. Used wisely, social media can be a tremendous tool for relaxation, fellowship, business networking, and ministering to others. Used carelessly, it can be a distraction and a hindrance to focusing on your family and other priorities. Remember the value of your time and use your time online with discretion and self-discipline.

Balance Accessibility and Boundaries

It's hard enough to handle technological interruptions wisely, but the stakes are much higher when dealing with our children. Children are a blessing, and we need to fight the temptation to think of their interruptions as a burden. It's important to be available to our kids, but they also need to learn age-appropriate boundaries. In chapter 10, we'll explore how to teach children responsibility, independence, initiative, and service—all of which will help them honor the boundaries we'll discuss here.

Spending more time with your family is a major benefit of homeschooling; running a home business often has a similar motivation. Ironically, when you're at home almost all the time, you can easily slip into the habit of being there but not really there because you're distracted, frustrated, and overwhelmed. We've looked at lots of ways to counteract those challenges, but there's another important strategy to consider: balancing accessibility with boundaries.

> Learning about accessibility and boundaries has revolutionized my whole life. As my therapist once said, "Holly, you are a very accommodating person. If a workman was doing house repairs and he asked you to step out to the yard and talk, you would stand there for forty-five minutes and not even realize you were having sunstroke."
> HOLLY NELSON, Kansas

Establish Boundaries of Time

Being accessible doesn't mean being available on demand at all times. Of course, this depends on the ages of your children and how many you have. If you have an infant or all your children are preschoolers, your approach will be quite different from that of a mother of teens. As your children grow older and more independent, gradually draw some boundaries around your time and teach your children to respect them.

At the same time, be sensitive to important interruptions. Sometimes a child really does need attention and can't wait. Generally the younger the child, the less he can wait. Use discernment and realize that sometimes a child's need for your immediate attention or assistance is more important than whatever else you are trying to focus on.

Including children in the housework and your home business, if you have one, is a great way to extend your accessibility, but we all need some uninterrupted time for lesson planning, work, reflection, Bible study, and the occasional sanity break.

Many families set aside the morning for homeschooling, especially for lessons that require parental instruction or one-on-one assistance. Afternoons are then dedicated to independent lessons, chores, and free time for the children while mom works on her business, volunteer work, or household tasks. Other families save some homeschool lessons for the evening so Dad can participate. One of my friends goes to bed early while her children stay up late. She then gets up early to work on her home business while they sleep late, and they all meet for lessons at 10:00 a.m. This system works well for their family. The important thing is to find out what works for *your* family.

Moms who have a home business often work early in the morning before the children wake up, during their nap time, or after they go to bed. These can be great opportunities to set aside some uninterrupted work time, but make sure you're not routinely sacrificing your own sleep. If that's the only uninterrupted time you have, use those precious quiet hours for the kind of work that requires concentrated thought, like writing or studying. When the kids are awake, use that interruption-prone time for more routine tasks like bill paying, packing and shipping, or checking e-mail.

> One of the best things about teaching at home is that it gives you the ability to tailor your time to suit the needs of you and your children. Creativity requires time and space. When Michael is writing an album or a book, he is always seeking large blocks of uninterrupted time. . . . Interruptions can break into your concentration and focus, because creating original work is an exhausting process of trial and error that requires time and space.
>
> SUSAN CARD
> *The Homeschool Journey*

Try to work in designated blocks of time so the children know when you'll be available. I typically work in my home office for an hour at a time. (Back pain prevents me from sitting at the computer for longer than that.) I tell the kids, "I'm getting ready to work now. I'll be at my computer for an hour. Do you need anything from me?" I give them all their assignments and supplies for the entire week on Monday, but if they need specific items or have questions about what to do next, I can take care of them before I start working. Then they won't interrupt my work to say, "I'm not sure what I'm supposed to be doing now" or "You didn't give me the math test."

Teach older children to pause before interrupting you—especially during a designated time for focused work—and think about how they would handle the situation if you weren't there. If I'm napping, my boys won't wake me unless there's an emergency. But when I'm working in my home office, I seem more available, so they're likelier to come in the minute they have a question. I finally told them, "If you wouldn't wake me up if I were taking a nap, don't interrupt my work. Think about what would you do if I were asleep."

My twelve-year-old recently started looking at my computer when he wants to ask me something. If he sees Facebook or e-mail on the screen, he'll talk to me. But if I have a Word document open, he knows I'm probably editing, so he leaves the room quietly and lets me know what he needs the next time I come out. Because I've trained him to be independent and responsible, he can usually manage until then, or a big brother can help him. But he also knows that if it's urgent, he can tell me right away and I'll be happy to help him.

Establish Boundaries of Space

You need boundaries of space as well as time. Doing as much as possible in the family room or kitchen is a great way to make yourself accessible, and laptop computers or tablets facilitate that. However, mental concentration thrives on solitude and silence. I'm focusing primarily on home business in this section, but you can apply these strategies in other areas of your life such as lesson planning, volunteer work, or personal devotions.

Establishing boundaries of space means being physically separated from your children sometimes. This seems contradictory for a home-and-family-based lifestyle, doesn't it? But having some quiet, concentrated time will allow you to work more efficiently, which then frees you to enjoy more focused time with your family.

If you work from home, try to designate a separate office area—preferably a separate room so you can close the door when necessary. In large families or small houses, this may not be possible, but think creatively and see if you can come up with a solution. One friend set up his office in his home's large foyer. Working in your bedroom is not ideal, but sometimes it's the best or only option available. Putting up a free-standing folding screen can create a visual barrier and a greater sense of a separate space.

> Having my desk in the living room worked well in our previous home because I could send the girls to their rooms and not be distracted while I was working on website design. The way our current house is set up, there's no privacy whatsoever in the living room. Moving my office to my bedroom has been such a big help. I can shut the door and concentrate and get much more done. It also serves as a retreat when I'm not working.
> JANET WILFRED, Georgia

I have been blessed with a four-bedroom house. My four sons share two bedrooms so that I can use the master bedroom as my office. It holds two desks, five filing cabinets, and eighteen bookcases (some of them backed up against my desk in the middle of the room). Having a separate room helps eliminate distractions so I can concentrate on editing, writing, and coaching. Being able to literally shut the door also helps keep me from getting sucked back into work when I need to be with my family. I am very thankful for my home office. Although I use it primarily when I need to be undisturbed, I sometimes invite one of my sons to do his schoolwork in there while I'm working—whoever needs the most accountability or the most encouragement at the time.

Whether or not you have a home office, sometimes it's useful to leave your house for a concentrated time of work or planning. Some bloggers do much of their writing at coffee shops. When my children were very young, I would sometimes leave them at our house with their dad or a babysitter, and I would go to the library, the park, or the nearby Mexican restaurant (which I used to call my office away from home) to write or edit. The background noise at restaurants doesn't distract me because none of it requires my attention. I was not immediately available to my children, but there was an adult in charge, and I was less than a mile away if I were needed at home. My boys are now old enough to be at home alone, and I still do some of my best thinking and writing at restaurants or the library. A change of environment often provides a creative breakthrough for writer's block.

If you can't or don't want to leave the house, consider hiring a mother's helper while you're at home. You can use a younger sitter because you're there to handle emergencies. For years I hired several homeschooled girls who were a wonderful blessing to our family. I would nurse the baby and then go upstairs to work on my Fitzgerald book. Kathy or Molly or Kathryn would change diapers, cook lunch, wash dishes, fold laundry, play with the children, or take them for a walk. This strategy works especially well when your children are young.

When you can't leave or hire help, provide your children with activities to keep them occupied while you're busy. This works best with older children. They can play outside, play in another room, play computer games, watch a short video, do chores inside or outside, work on homeschool lessons, read books of their own choosing, play board games, build with LEGO blocks, draw, and much more. Check on them frequently and teach them not to interrupt you except for emergencies.

Is It Really an Emergency?

If you want your children to refrain from interrupting you, it's essential that you define what constitutes an emergency. "I want LEGOs for Christmas" is not an emergency. "Can I have a Batman birthday party next year?" is not an emergency. "I want to be a doctor when I grow up" is not an emergency. The problem is that the list of the things that do *not* constitute an emergency is infinite.

I began by defining *emergency* as something involving blood, fire, or water, but I quickly realized I had to be more specific. Blood means a gaping head wound, not an easily bandaged fingertip where the cat scratched you. Water does not mean a small puddle on the kitchen floor where somebody dropped an ice cube and it melted. It means water is pouring through the ceiling fan in the living room because the stopper was left in the upstairs sink, the faucet was dripping, and the entire family left the house for three hours. (Ask me how I know about that one.)

I always thought fire was fairly straightforward, but apparently it's not. One winter day, I was happily editing in my office and thinking, "Wow, the kids are being so good! I'm getting so much done!" After a while I started hearing some noise and thought, "They're getting kind of rowdy, but they'd let me know if there was a problem, so I guess everything's OK." The noise kept escalating, however, so I decided I'd better see what was going on.

When I came out of my office, the kids were in hysterics. I could hardly understand what they were saying. Finally, one managed to gasp, "Snoball is on fire!"

Snoball was one of our cats who loved to stretch out blissfully on the rug in front of our woodstove. A spark had popped out and landed on his back, so he was racing around the house in terror. The kids were racing around Snoball, certain that their beloved pet was about to go up in flames.

I love our cats, but I was more concerned that the cat was going to ignite the furniture and that the *house* was going to go up in flames. Perry managed to trap Snoball under the sofa and extinguish the spark with his finger. His finger was only slightly scorched, and the cat was ultimately uninjured. You do *not* want to smell singed cat fur—trust me on this.

> In reality, all you can do is accept each day from the Lord, live it as wisely as possible, and stay flexible. Learn to expect inconvenient interruptions, incomplete goals, and time-eating bouts of immaturity in your children. Don't expect more of yourself than God does—faithfulness.
> CLAY AND SALLY CLARKSON
> *Educating the WholeHearted Child*

It took me half an hour to calm down the most hysterical animal lover. Finally, when everything settled down and the panic had passed, I asked, "What were you thinking? Why didn't you tell me the cat was on fire?!"

They looked at me and said with all sincerity, "We didn't want to interrupt your work."

No matter what boundaries you establish, no matter what rules you set up, no matter how well you try to define what is and is not an emergency, there's always some fine-tuning to do. But make sure that your kids know that a flaming cat is, in fact, an emergency.

Remember That God Is in Control

Sometimes interruptions happen despite your best-laid plans. Pray for discernment to know how to respond to each situation. Sometimes the appropriate response is to ignore an interruption and continue the task at hand. At other times, an interruption is a signal to be sensitive to God's timing and an opportunity to serve someone who really needs you. C. S. Lewis said, "What one calls the interruptions are precisely one's real life—the life God is sending one day by day."[1]

English nun Janet Erskine Stuart's attitude provides a wonderful reminder of how God's providence applies to interruptions. Her assistant explains:

> She delighted in seeing her plan upset by unexpected events, saying it gave her great comfort, and that she looked on such things as an assurance that God was watching over her stewardship, was securing the accomplishment of His will, and working out His own designs. Whether she traced the secondary causes to the prayer of a child, the imperfection of an individual, to obstacles arising from misunderstandings, or to interference of outside agencies, she was joyfully and gracefully ready to recognize the indication of God's ruling hand, and to allow herself to be guided by it.[2]

Take Action!

☐ How do you respond to interruptions? Think about your attitude and emotions as well as your outward response. What do you need to change about how you respond?

☐ What interruptions do you encounter most often?

☐ What can you do to avoid or prevent common interruptions? Think especially about setting boundaries for technological interruptions such as phone calls, texts, e-mail, and social media.

☐ How well do you balance accessibility and boundaries with your children? What changes do you need to make?

CHAPTER 8

It's Time for an Attitude Adjustment

Speak that word to me today, dear Lord: peace. Let Your calm spirit, through the many potentially rough minutes of this day, in every task, say to my soul, Be still. Even this day's chaos, with all its clutter and exertion, will be ordered by Your quiet power if my heart is subject to Your word of peace.
ELISABETH ELLIOT, *A Lamp Unto My Feet*

Guilt. Fear. Discouragement. Why did I keep slamming up against them while writing a book like this? It was scheduled to be published in 2013, not 2014, and I was on track—until I came down with a vicious bout of bronchitis and persistent sinusitis. Simply breathing consumed most of my energy, both physical and mental, for an entire month. By the time I had recovered enough to get back to work, a major editing client needed me to focus on her book instead of mine. When I finally returned to revising my own manuscript, I just couldn't get back in the groove. I complained to my family and close friends, and I was afraid of what people would think about the delay. In my head I knew I had practiced what I preach by taking care of myself, doing what I could do, and trying to find peace in the space between the ideal and reality. But my heart was consumed by guilt, and I felt like a fraud. Who would take my book about achieving balance seriously when I couldn't even finish the manuscript on time?

My dear friend and editor Zan Tyler let me pour out my angst, encouraged me, and then told me I should share this story. She reminded me that real life never goes away and neither do our emotions. Bad attitudes aren't something we deal with once and for all; instead, we have to make a choice every day to honor God with our thoughts and attitudes as well as our actions.

You may want to don your steel-toed boots for this chapter and the next because I might step on your toes. I'm certainly stepping on my own. Over the years I've discovered that I learn the most from people who challenge me and make me ask myself hard questions that I'd rather not face. Pause to pray before reading on and ask God to help you to be honest with yourself as you seek to identify attitudes and habits you may need to change.

Let Go of Guilt

The word *guilt* came up surprisingly often in a survey for my "How Do You Do It All?" class. In fact, it was the third most frequently used word after *time* and *balance*.

It's important to distinguish between true guilt and false guilt. Of course we should feel guilty when we sin. We should confess and repent. But moms are often consumed by false guilt triggered by comparisons and unrealistic expectations. "Mommy guilt" is so common that a recent Google search for the phrase yielded 5 million results. A mom may worry that she's shortchanging her kids somehow, that her house isn't clean enough, that her meals aren't nutritious enough, and so much more. And she feels guilty about *all* of it.

But one of the most common sources of mommy guilt seems to be taking time to take care of ourselves. Watch just a few minutes of television or scan the contents of an average magazine at the grocery checkout and you'll find ample evidence of people overindulging, being lazy, being selfish, and "taking care of Number One." It's also easy to swing too far to the other extreme and become paranoid about any hint of self-care. You've probably encountered at least one book, article, blog post, or speaker claiming that it's unreasonable or even sinful for moms to need rest or "me time." But there's no need to feel guilty if you're taking care of yourself wisely. Motherhood involves service and sacrifice, not martyrdom. There is a difference. As we'll see in chapter 9, taking care of yourself is necessary for you to be able to take care of your family.

> Motherhood is a very long-term calling and I think all women need the encouragement of other women that they should not feel guilty for taking a break once in a while when they are in need of some breathing room!
> SALLY CLARKSON

Don't let guilt be the thing that holds you down. Planning your life around the three basic categories of personal, family, and business and honestly evaluating them can keep you in balance and help you identify whether you're doing the right thing.

Bid Farewell to Fear

Twice in my life I have let irrational fears hold me back. These are two of the choices I've regretted most. When I was just out of college and working a secretarial job while my husband was in seminary, my father had the opportunity to spend time with Eudora Welty, one of my favorite writers. She was an alumna of the university where he worked, and he was going to a video interview with her. Only a few people would be there, and he said I could go with him, but I was afraid the crew wouldn't want me tagging along. I settled for sending a couple of my books with Dad for Miss Welty to sign. He got to chat with her for half an hour—and I could have been there. A few years later I did get to meet her very briefly and have her sign one of my books in person, but I still regret letting fear hold me back from that once-in-a-lifetime opportunity to have a real conversation with her.

> Naturally, it is the very breath of life . . . to go out and see what is to be seen of the world. For the artist to be unwilling to move, mentally or spiritually or physically, out of the familiar is a sign that spiritual timidity or poverty or decay has come upon him; for what is familiar will then have turned into all that is tyrannical.
>
> EUDORA WELTY
> "Place in Fiction"

The other time was when I was in graduate school. In 1991, I was working with the world's leading F. Scott Fitzgerald scholar on a new edition of *The Great Gatsby* for Cambridge University Press, an amazing opportunity that later helped me build my editing business. I was invited to the publication party at the historic Scribner Book Store in New York City. But I was pregnant with my first child, terrified of the big city, had never flown before, and was especially nervous because I didn't know how to hail a cab. So I didn't go.

The New York story has a happy ending. It just took eighteen years to get there! In 2009, I flew to Manhattan for Book Expo America, the publishing industry trade show. I was amazed to find the city invigorating, not terrifying. Everyone I met was friendly and helpful, including the cab drivers. When I went back to the Book Expo in 2010, I confidently took buses and cabs everywhere I wanted to go. I even walked down Broadway—alone—from the Flatiron District through Soho and Little Italy all the way to Chinatown.

I share these stories to encourage you not to let your fears cause regret, but to go for the things that make you a little—or even very—uncomfortable. If you're contemplating something that makes you afraid, ask yourself, "What's the worst that could happen?" If the worst thing that could happen is that you won't accomplish what you set out to do, go ahead and give it a try. If you don't succeed, you're no worse off than you were without trying. But if you do succeed, you're better off.

Put Away Perfectionism

It's a bit ironic for an editor to list perfectionism as a potential hindrance, but I promised to be real. One homeschool mom told me, "I would like to be more willing and less afraid to make mistakes." Don't let fear of making mistakes keep you from trying. Get out of your comfort zone and try something new. There will never be a perfect time, so don't wait for it. You'll never achieve perfection, so aim for excellence instead.

If you take art lessons, you'll draw a lot of crooked lines and paint a lot of disappointing messes before you create something beautiful. If you learn to play the piano, you'll hit a lot of discordant notes before you're able to perform a Rachmaninoff concerto. But if you'll learn from your mistakes and keep practicing, you'll achieve excellence over time.

When I taught my live "How Do You Do It All?" class, I knew the teleseminar wouldn't go perfectly—technological glitches are almost inevitable. I knew the material wasn't perfectly organized, despite my best efforts. But I also knew that the class would help real people with real problems, so I pushed ahead with it. If I had waited for perfection, I would have missed out on the blessing of helping hundreds of moms. And most likely, I would never have written this book.

> Twenty years from now you will be more disappointed by the things you didn't do than by the ones you did do. So throw off the bowlines. Sail away from the safe harbor. Catch the trade winds in your sails. Explore. Dream. Discover.
> Attributed to MARK TWAIN

Perfectionism is the mother of procrastination. I've noticed that the more important or complicated a task is, the likelier I am to put it off until I have more time to deal with it thoroughly. This wouldn't be a bad idea if I got back to these tasks soon, but too often I continue putting them off—sometimes until it's so late that it would be embarrassing to do them at all. It would be much better to go ahead and handle them as best I can than to neglect them altogether. This is an area I'm still working on.

Don't allow perfectionism to paralyze you. Don't wait until your house is spotless to invite friends over for dinner. Don't bother ironing your little boys' clothes. (As a wise friend told me, it's hard to notice wrinkles on a moving target.) Don't search so long for one "perfect" math curriculum that you don't start math until three months into the school year. Learn to accept when good enough is good enough.

Wave Goodbye to Whining

Remember my "no whining" rule? Complaining drains your energy and keeps you from doing what God has called you to do. The cure for whining is to find peace in the space between the ideal and reality. Face the circumstances of your life and find a way to live out your priorities anyway.

The very week I was teaching about these bad attitudes in my class, I test-drove another mistake. After Wednesday night Bible study at church, my seven-year-old asked to do another phonics lesson. Doesn't that sound great? But I had already spent all day on homeschooling (including phonics) and other family responsibilities, and I had scheduled the time after church for work, so I told him no. He started whining, actually *begging* for more phonics. I was determined to get to my work, and I ended up snapping at him. Of course, then I was frustrated with myself, I felt guilty, and I wound up having a mini-meltdown of my own. I wasted more time on that pity party than I would have spent if I'd actually sat down and done another phonics lesson with him or if I had simply said no and corrected his attitude without adding a bad attitude of my own.

> Feelings, like thoughts, must be brought into captivity. No one whose first concern is feeling good can be a disciple.
> ELISABETH ELLIOT
> *Discipline: The Glad Surrender*

Just remember that no matter how much you practice these strategies—no matter how much balance you think you've achieved—you're always going to be tempted to give in to the feeling of being overwhelmed. You just have to deal with it the best you can and remember that God is in control.

Reject Resentment

Whining focuses on what you dislike about your own life; resentment focuses on what you envy in someone else's life. Envy is ugly—and much more common in our lives than we'd like to admit.

Keep those steel-toed boots on and examine your heart honestly: Have you ever envied another mom? Have you resented something she has that you lack, such as a supportive husband, lavish vaca-tions, more children, fewer children, housekeeping help, an ample book budget, free time, music lessons for her children, beautiful clothes, a bigger house, a nicer neighborhood, good health, boundless energy, or help from her extended family?

> Contentment is essentially a matter of accepting from God's hand what He sends because we know that He is good and therefore it is good.
>
> J. I. PACKER

So often we don't know about other people's struggles. The apparently abundant life of your local Supermom may hide challenges you can't even imagine. She may need your compassion, not your envy.

Contentment is the cure for resentment. We must rejoice in the good things that others have and be grateful for what we have. As the apostle Paul reminds us, "Godliness with contentment is great gain" (1 Timothy 6:6, NIV).

Set Aside Self-Righteousness

Homeschool moms can be a fairly judgmental lot. Whether we admit it or not, it can be tempting to look down on other families who choose to send their children away from home to be educated. This attitude is apparent in many of our conversations, blog posts, Facebook statuses, and more. I've been guilty of it myself. Sometimes we judge within our homeschooling circles even more viciously. How many arguments have you seen—or participated in—about educational philosophy, methods, and curriculum, not to mention issues like birthing, breastfeeding, discipline, cooking, how to dress, entertainment choices, and more?

The more strongly committed you are to something, the more enthusiastic you naturally are to urge other people to do the same thing so they can enjoy the same benefits. With the right attitude, sharing information and encouraging people to explore new options can be helpful. On the other hand, being judgmental and laying a burden of guilt on those who have made different decisions for their families only hurts others and turns them away. It's a delicate balance, but deep inside, you know your own attitude and motivations.

> We should beware rigidity in our orbit, and also legalism in criticizing the orbit of another. The secret of balance is not found in enforced uniformity and legalistic rigidity. Instead it is achieved, first, in placing durable priorities at the center of our existence, and, second, placing our lives in a stable orbit around these same priorities.
> RICHARD A. SWENSON, MD
> *In Search of Balance*

The reverse is also true: It's easy to be hypersensitive and assume that others are judging you because you're doing something different than they are. How often has a public-school mom quickly explained her educational choice the moment you mention that you homeschool? Right or wrong, she may assume that you're judging her just because your different choice makes her uncomfortable. If you're an unschooler, perhaps you automatically go on the defensive in any conversation with a classical homeschooler. Or vice versa. I used to be annoyed when store clerks asked my children, "Why aren't you in school today?" My sons, however, usually offered a simple, friendly explanation that they are homeschooled. I was amazed at how often a clerk responded positively, sometimes even by mentioning friends and family who homeschooled, and I was thankful I held my tongue.

When someone asks why you homeschool, do you automatically assume she's criticizing you? Before responding, consider whether she is hostile, simply curious, genuinely concerned for your family's well-being, or perhaps even testing the waters to consider homeschooling for her own family. It's usually better not to engage in a debate with those who are truly hostile, but to have a simple, brief answer ready—something along the lines of "This is what I believe is best for my family"—and leave it at that. On the other hand, if someone seems genuinely interested, you might want to go into a bit more detail than you would with someone who's merely looking to pick a fight. Dealing with the simply curious falls somewhere in the middle. The genuinely concerned (family members, perhaps, or your pastor) deserve a thoughtful reply.

Be gracious and give others the benefit of the doubt. Don't jump to conclusions, and don't pound people on the head with your own choices.

Say No to Negativity

Have you ever been around someone who is consistently grumpy or complaining? Even a brief encounter with a rude or negative person can put a damper on your day or rub off on your own attitude. On the other hand, a cheerful person can encourage you and lift your spirits when you're feeling down. Deborah, a server at a restaurant where I occasionally enjoy a Saturday breakfast, is always smiling, friendly, and upbeat. Just being around her energizes me and gets my day off to a good start.

Remember that your attitude—positive or negative—is an example for your children and sets the tone for your entire household. You know the old saying: "If Mama ain't happy, ain't nobody happy!" Edith Schaeffer expresses this in terms of creating an environment for the people around us:

> Our conversations, attitudes, behavior, response or lack of response, hardness or compassion, our love or selfishness, joy or dullness, our demonstrated trust and faith or our continual despondency, our concern for others or our self pity—all these things make a difference to the people who have to live in our "environment." Enthusiasm and excitement infect other people: expectancy that God can intervene and do something in this moment of history and doing something practical to show that expectancy in prayer, affects the attitudes other people are going to have to their troubles.[1]

As an overwhelmed new mom, I often focused on the negative. When we had a hard day, I blew it out of proportion and tended to think that most days would be equally rough. On the other hand, when we had a great day, I saw it as an exception. How much better that first year would have been if I had reversed those attitudes and focused on the good instead of the bad!

When you face a challenge, do you naturally think, "I can't do this," or do you ask yourself, "How can I do this?" As we saw in chapter 2, asking "How can I?" rather than saying "I can't" opens your mind to

> I am still determined to be cheerful and happy in whatever situation I may be; for I have also learned from experience that the greater part of our happiness or misery depends upon our dispositions and not upon our circumstances.
>
> MARTHA WASHINGTON

the possibilities and keeps your focus positive rather than negative. That's a huge mental shift, and it made a big difference for me once I learned to think that way.

Take Action!

☐ If you found yourself squirming—or becoming annoyed—as you read any part of this chapter, that's likely a sign of conviction. Examine your heart honestly. Do you need to correct any of these attitudes?

- Guilt

- Fear

- Perfectionism

- Whining

- Resentment

- Self-Righteousness

- Negativity

Pray for God's help as you seek to adjust your attitude.

CHAPTER 9

Oxygen Masks and Monkey Bread Days

Rest time is not waste time. It is economy to gather fresh strength. . . .
It is wisdom to take occasional furlough. In the long run, we shall do
more by sometimes doing less.
CHARLES HADDON SPURGEON

Homeschooling moms are not known for taking good care of ourselves. In fact, this is one of the major problem areas that has come up over and over again in my surveys. Here are some of the challenges moms have shared with me:

- I feel overwhelmed.

- I need to stop worrying.

- I don't know what to do about interruptions and distractions.

- I feel pulled in several directions all the time.

- I never slow down during the day, but I don't feel like I'm getting enough done.

- I want to make time for myself without feeling guilty about it.

- I lack focus.

- I lack confidence.

- I don't have time to exercise.

- I don't have time to rest.

- I often have a sinking feeling.

You've probably faced many of these challenges yourself.

Have you ever had a day when it seems everyone wants a piece of you? I call these monkey bread days. Monkey bread is a delicious cinnamon bread made up of little chunks to be pulled off by hand and devoured. It's also a great image of the life of a homeschooling mom. So many people are pulling at you until eventually you have nothing left to give. Storing up reserves in advance by taking care of yourself equips you to cope with these monkey bread days with grace.

A wise nineteenth-century author observed:

How many a woman's life is spoilt by the fret and fever of a disquieted spirit waiting for "more time," and feeling the overwhelming claim of home life, upon every moment of her day, she gets in the stream of ceaseless work and worry, and denies herself the necessary leisure for physical recreations and spiritual rest! . . . Duties never clash. If thoughtful mothers would remember their "previous claims" upon time and energy and strength, they would not rob their lives of the quiet and rest which health of soul and body alike demand by accepting responsibilities which are too often burdensome and at best but ill-discharged.[1]

Put On Your Oxygen Mask

When you're pregnant, nobody rebukes you for taking care of yourself because they realize that the only way you can take care of that precious little person growing inside your body is to take care of yourself. But when the baby is born and the cord is cut, the focus completely shifts, and it no longer seems quite so acceptable to take care of yourself. Of course, your main focus is the new baby, but if you neglect yourself, you'll eventually burn out and crash, and you won't be able to take care of anybody. The same is true no matter how old your children are.

> When we insist on living overloaded lives, this choice not only damages our own well-being, but also inflicts damage on those around us.
> RICHARD A. SWENSON, MD
> *The Overload Syndrome*

You know the flight attendant's advice: Put on your *own* oxygen mask first. If you deal with the struggling child first, you may pass out before you get your own mask on, and then you won't be able to help anybody.

Don't forget that how you handle interruptions, challenges, and frustrations and how you take care of yourself (or fail to do so) create a model for your children. Your actions speak louder than words. What message are you sending your kids as they form habits for their own lives? Don't set them on a path that leads to their own burnout someday. Instead, set an example of a well-balanced life so that you—and they—can flourish.

Nourish Your Spiritual Life

Susanna Wesley, the mother of nineteen children including the famous preachers John and Charles, threw her apron over her head when she wanted to pray. In this way she trained her children not to disturb her time with God.

Are you nourishing your spiritual life? Make it a priority to spend time with God each day through Bible reading and prayer—first thing in the morning, if possible. This helps you focus on God's way of doing things. As Charles Spurgeon said, "It is well frequently to weigh ourselves in the scale of God's Word."[2] It also serves as a reminder of your dependence on God: "My help comes from the Lord, who made heaven and earth" (Psalm 121:2, ESV).

This is another example of not waiting for someday to do what matters most. Maybe you've heard of someone who spends two hours in prayer every morning, and you're discouraged because you can't do the same. Don't let the lack of ideal circumstances keep you from doing the important thing now. If you have young children, your devotional time may have to

> Reading the Scriptures shuts out worldly cares, dulls carnal delights, and enflames divine love. It steers the judgment, clears the memory, cheers the conscience, and sweetly composes the affections.
> ROBERT DINGLEY
> Puritan preacher

come in small chunks throughout the day. You can memorize Scripture by writing a verse on some index cards and putting them on the dryer, above the kitchen sink, or over the baby's changing table. Read it aloud a few times while going about your work, and soon you'll know it by heart.

Keep a Sabbath one day a week by refraining from your usual work. Not only does this honor God, but it also refreshes you to accomplish more in the other six days.

I've finally learned to rest! I'm taking an electronic Sabbath, which has helped so much! I was working 24/7 and woke up Monday mornings emotionally drained. Now I'm taking Sunday off, and I'm refreshed and energized come Monday morning in time for my busy week.
RITA JOHNSON, Illinois

Build time into your life for fellowship with other people who share your spiritual beliefs, and don't neglect corporate worship. Hebrews 10:24–25 reminds us "to stimulate one another to love and good deeds, not forsaking our own assembling together, as is the habit of some, but encouraging one another; and all the more as you see the day drawing near."

In addition to maintaining regular times for private and public worship, remember that you can and should serve and glorify God with every aspect of your daily life. Keep in mind these encouraging words from seventeenth-century French monk Brother Lawrence:

The time of business does not with me differ from the time of prayer, and in the noise and clatter of my kitchen, while several persons are at the same time calling for different things, I possess God in as great tranquility as if I were upon my knees at the blessed sacrament.[3]

You Can't Trade In Your Burned-Out Body for a Newer Model

I've had back trouble for many years. Long hours of writing and editing on the computer only exacerbate the problem. Regular visits to the chiropractor help limit my pain and keep me functioning well, but driving to the clinic, waiting, getting adjusted, and doing various therapies are time-consuming. On an especially busy Friday, I thought, "I just don't have time today to go to the chiropractor," so I canceled my appointment. My pain became so much worse that I couldn't complete the urgent work after all. I hadn't saved time; I had lost it.

Taking care of my health is an ongoing challenge for me. I have been an indulgent eater and indifferent exerciser for most of my life, making only sporadic efforts to improve my habits. The stress of single motherhood has added to the toll on my mind and body, and I've walked around foggy-headed and exhausted far too long. A few years ago, I received a wake-up call when extensive lab work revealed just how much damage had been done to my adrenal glands, my thyroid, my blood sugar balance, and my heart. I've had to make some major lifestyle changes, and it hasn't been easy.

With all your many responsibilities as a busy homeschool mom, it's easy to neglect your own health, sometimes without even realizing you're doing so. Skipping exercise and sleep may seem like practical ways to save time, but ultimately

> God gave us an amazing gift, and all we are required to do is feed it, water it, rest it, and move it. Yet it needs to be the right food, water, rest, and movement. If we perform our assignment well, we will find energy we never knew we had. We will work better, run better, feel better, heal better, and live better.
> RICHARD A. SWENSON, MD
> *Margin*

you're sabotaging your ability to do the things you really care about. In fact, many chronic illnesses can be traced to years of poor nutrition, insufficient exercise, too much stress, and inadequate sleep.

Whether you're dealing with serious, chronic health challenges or you've just gotten used to ignoring your health, please resolve to make taking care of yourself a high priority. Evaluate your habits in the areas of nutrition, hydration, exercise, and sleep and set appropriate goals for making necessary changes. Be sure not to tackle too many things at once, but focus on a steady progression of making small changes for the better. As with the rest of your life, your children will learn more by your example than by your words.

Use the personal category of your weekly goals to hold yourself accountable in these areas. If you need help, consider sharing your goals with others. As I mentioned earlier, reporting to my mastermind team about taking my nutritional supplements really helped me build this important habit.

Put the Right Fuel in Your Engine

Once I accidentally put watered-down gas in my van, and it died on the side of the highway, leaving my four boys and me stranded. Just like an engine needs the right fuel to run, our bodies need the right nutrition to function properly.

I know many moms who love to cook, but I'm not one of them. Frankly, I often begrudge the time it takes to prepare a healthy meal. At one time, I should have bought stock in Hamburger Helper! This is another area where you have to find the right balance between the ideal and reality. For example, I'm trying to minimize my family's use of canned vegetables (so convenient) and use more frozen and fresh produce. Our gardening attempts have been a flop in our soggy, shady soil, so we buy fresh vegetables at the grocery store or farmer's market. However, I still keep our pantry stocked with canned goods for weather emergencies and super-busy days.

Canning produce and baking from scratch can be healthy, economical, and delicious, but they are also time consuming. Figure out what works best for your family, and don't take on a burden of false guilt just because you don't prepare meals like Supermom.

Many excellent books on nutrition are available. Use them to educate yourself and then take action on what you learn.

Stay Hydrated

I used to think of drinking water as a burden—a healthy obligation I had to chug down, like it or not. But the more I drank it, the more I enjoyed it. My attitude toward water was changed when I began to learn about how many different parts of the world don't have ready access to clean water. A friend who visited missionaries in Mexico told me how painstakingly they had to ration water, even for brushing their teeth—something I took utterly for granted.

To symbolize my new attitude toward water, I bought a vintage etched crystal goblet at an antique store. Every time I drink from it, I remember what a blessing a clean water supply is. It also reminds me that even as we age, with proper care, we can remain beautiful, useful, and sparkling!

Dehydration is a factor in many health problems. Drinking enough water can increase your energy, improve your digestion, enhance mental clarity, help control your appetite, make your skin smoother, and relieve headaches and joint pain. How much water should you drink? It varies with exercise, environment, and health, but a common rule of thumb is eight cups a day.

Exercise

When you're weary and overwhelmed, sometimes just getting out of bed seems hard enough. But regular exercise gives you more energy and helps you face your daily challenges with a better attitude. It also prevents and minimizes many illnesses, improves sleep, controls weight, relieves stress, and makes it easier to learn and remember.

Many of my homeschool-mom friends love to run. In fact, several of them run marathons. Just reading their Facebook posts can be exhausting. It would suit me just fine never to work up a sweat again in my life, but I understand how important exercise is, and I've experienced the benefits when I've been diligent about walking or working out.

Walking is a great exercise for moms. It doesn't require special equipment, membership fees, or a specific schedule. You can push the baby in a stroller while your older kids walk alongside you or ride their bikes. You can walk with a friend for accountability and fellowship. Or you can walk alone for some much-needed quiet or prayer time. I've done all of these.

> She girds herself with strength and makes her arms strong.
> PROVERBS 31:17

I began by walking twenty minutes (about one mile) three to five days a week, then raised my goal to thirty minutes five days a week. When I'm walking regularly, I feel so much better. I have more energy, my back pain is reduced, and my productivity increases. It's also a great way to relieve tension and frustration. Sometimes if I'm upset or tired, going out for a short walk is just the refreshing break I need to get me back on track.

Whether you run, walk, go to the gym, swim, or something else, find a type of exercise that suits your abilities and your schedule and gradually make it a priority.

Don't Sacrifice Sleep

One of my dearest friends was involved in a car wreck as she and her son were driving home late at night while they were sleepy. They veered off the road, ran over a stop sign, rolled over in a ditch, and landed three yards from an oak tree. She broke a couple of ribs and gashed the back of her head, and her son's hand was jammed. They could easily have been killed, but God spared their lives.

> Have courage for the great sorrows of life and patience for the small ones; and when you have laboriously accomplished your daily task, go to sleep in peace. God is awake.
> VICTOR HUGO

Getting by on as little sleep as possible is a common way for busy moms to find more hours in their day, but it should be the exception rather than the rule. Most adults need seven to eight hours of sleep per night. If you don't get that regularly, your health will surely suffer. Chronic sleep deprivation impairs memory and concentration, reduces alertness, increases irritability, causes poor judgment, contributes to weight gain, weakens your immune system, and increases your risk of high blood pressure and other serious health problems.

If you have an infant or many young children, you may be ready to throw this book across the room. Sleeping eight hours a night may sound like a fantasy. It's definitely a challenge, and there are no easy answers. Remember that infancy is only a short season and do the best you can to get the rest you need—yet another place where you must find peace in the space between the ideal and reality. A dear friend told me she often prayed for other mothers who were up with their children in the middle of the night. Just knowing that other women were doing the same thing really helped her attitude.

Taking a nap is a good way to supplement your nighttime sleep. Nap when the baby naps and your older children rest or have a quiet play time. Napping isn't just a strategy for tired moms. British Prime Minister Winston Churchill took an afternoon nap for at least an hour every day during World War II. In his memoirs, he explained, "Nature had not intended mankind to work from eight in the morning until midnight without the refreshment of blessed oblivion which, even if it only lasts twenty minutes, is sufficient to renew all the vital forces. I regretted having to send myself to bed like a child every afternoon, but I was rewarded by being able to work through the night until two or even later—sometimes much later—in the morning, and begin the new day between eight and nine o'clock. This routine I observed throughout the war, and I commend it to others if and when they find it necessary for a long spell to get the last scrap out of the human structure."[4]

> The single most important thing I've learned is to give myself permission to take a nap, or at least lie down, midway during the day. When I take this dedicated rest time, I not only rest physically, but I can also use the time to focus, reflect, and dream. From napping, I have developed the ability to rest in other ways, such as connecting with God every day, enjoying a routine Sabbath without apology, and even developing a much-needed support network.
> HOLLY NELSON, Kansas

Build a Support Network

In my second year of homeschooling, a friend and I and our children met for lunch at a playground. While we were there, we met another mom with a school-age child and found out she was homeschooling too. As we chatted, this other mom commented that she wasn't a part of a support group because she didn't need any help. Formal support groups aren't for everyone, but we all need some kind of help and support.

Make sure that you build a support network of people who can encourage you on a regular basis and help you in emergencies—and do the same for them. Especially when you're doing something as countercultural as homeschooling, spending time with likeminded friends can be refreshing, motivating, and inspiring.

> Iron sharpens iron, so one man sharpens another.
> PROVERBS 27:17

Homeschool support groups and co-ops are good places to find friends who share your values. Even when you don't especially feel like you need to go, remember that other mothers there may need your advice and encouragement. Homeschool Mom's Night Out has been a regular monthly commitment for me for many years. Even during especially busy times when I'm tempted to skip it, I return home refreshed and more productive. Church is a great place to build strong relationships based on your shared faith. Look for what you have in common with others rather than what divides you—don't limit your friendships to other homeschoolers.

Real-life friendships are the most important, but you can also find kindred spirits in online discussion groups and on Facebook. Some people criticize these as artificial substitutes for the real thing, but I've developed many strong friendships online and have even had the opportunity to meet some of these friends in person, some-times after many years.

If you have a home business, it's essential that you network with other entrepreneurs. People who don't work at home often don't un-derstand the unique challenges of this lifestyle. Finding others to brainstorm, solve problems, and share ideas is priceless. I've made many lifelong friends at business conferences. These are also great places to find accountability partners and mastermind teammates.

Don't wait until there is an unusual need or emergency to begin building a support network. Even if you prefer not to hire babysitters, for example, it's a good idea to have a few friends you can trust with your children and with whom your children are familiar and comfortable. If you don't have extended family nearby, you might swap childcare with a friend occasionally for a date night with your husband or an afternoon alone.

In 2006, I went to Colorado for a business trip, and it took a relay of six different teams of people to replace me for six days. One family kept the kids overnight, while somebody else took them to our homeschool co-op the next day. They spent a few days with grandparents, and then a young couple from our church came to our house, and so on. All these people already knew my children well. This trip, which had a profound impact on the growth of my home business and thus on the well-being of our family, would not have been possible if those relationships had not already been in place.

Have Fun!

Are you doing anything just for the fun of it?

When I ask homeschool moms, "What's currently missing in your life that you'd like to make time for?" their replies include fun, hobbies, exercise, time alone, time with their husbands, time with their kids, recreation, time to read, time in nature, more artsy pursuits, travel with their families, barbecues, gardening, and sunsets.

> When you play, play hard; when you work, don't play at all.
> THEODORE ROOSEVELT

What's missing in your life that you'd like to make time for?

Everyone needs a break. Look for ways to build fun, recreation, and relaxation into your life. One mom told me, "I do stuff to relax and unwind, but it all seems so unproductive. I just tend to fall back on it because it's easy and familiar, and I don't have to think about what to do." Recreation doesn't necessarily have to be productive. Sometimes you need to cut loose and have some fun; sometimes you just need to relax. Take a few minutes to enjoy the beauty of God's creation. Stop and smell the roses or gaze at the clouds or listen to the birds.

When I'm traveling for business, I always try to include some sightseeing. If I've already driven several hours or paid for a plane ticket to a part of the country I've never been to, I'll add another day or two to explore and see another part of the country. (Note: The pleasure portion of a business trip is not tax-deductible.) My Big Dream list includes several places I want to visit, and business trips have taken me to several of those destinations, including Colorado and the Grand Canyon. What a blessing!

You don't have to leave home to have fun. Hobbies may sound like a joke to really busy people, but it's rewarding to do something just because you love it. I enjoy photography, scrapbooking, and cross-stitch, but reading is my primary recreation.

Having fun doesn't have to be expensive or time consuming. Think about activities you enjoy—maybe ones you've been neglecting—and look for ways to build them into your life a little at a time.

Take Action!

☐ How are you nourishing your spiritual life?

☐ How well are you taking care of your body? Consider how you need to improve in the following areas and make a commitment to do so.
  - Nutrition
  - Hydration
  - Exercise
  - Sleep

❐ Do you have a strong support network? If not, how can you establish one?

❐ What's currently missing in your life that you'd like to make time for? Schedule at least an hour to do it this week. This may be a bigger challenge than you realize, but it's worth the effort to make it happen.

CHAPTER 10

Training Your Children

How can it be a large career to tell other people's children about the rule of three, and a small career to tell one's own children about the universe? How can it be broad to be the same thing to everyone, and narrow to be everything to someone? No. A woman's function is laborious, but because it is gigantic, not because it is minute.

G. K. CHESTERTON

In her 1990 commencement speech at Wellesley College, Barbara Bush said, "At the end of your life, you will never regret not having passed one more test, not winning one more verdict, or not closing one more deal. You will regret time not spent with a husband, a child, a friend, or a parent."[1]

As a homeschooling mom, you've clearly made your family a

top priority, yet a busy life can sometimes shove family relationships onto the back burner despite your best intentions. Even the wise strategies we've been discussing for efficiency, productivity, and time management can backfire if you neglect to nurture your relationships and make your home a haven for your family.

Family relationships can bring us great satisfaction and personal rewards. For example, I love teaching my children when they get excited about a topic and want to pursue it. One homeschool mom told me she enjoys being able to go and do and play with her husband and girls when they're available. ("They have busy lives, and I want to be available when they are.") One mom with a home business said she enjoys accomplishing tasks, but talking with her son about spiritual things is "the most satisfying of all, to give him my undivided attention and have him share his heart."

Conversely, many homeschool moms also mention relationships as being among their biggest challenges. One mother told me she has always enjoyed her children on a daily basis and has felt blessed and joyful with them, but lately her joy is being sapped by an overwhelming sense of not getting done what needs to be done. A mom in the empty nest stage said her biggest challenge is letting her children make their own mistakes after they're grown up; she finds this even harder than their early baby days. Another mom struggles with giving her kids the attention they need while not pushing them too hard.

We'll take the next few chapters to explore ways to flourish in your family life. In this chapter we'll look at training your children. Many wonderful books about child training are available. Frankly, there's no way to cover the subject fully in a single chapter, so I'll focus on four things to teach your children that contribute greatly to building a balanced life for the whole family: responsibility, independence, initiative, and service.

Teach Your Children Responsibility

Having real responsibilities helps children build confidence, character, and a biblical self-image. They can find great satisfaction in making a meaningful contribution to the work of the family.

One of my favorite examples of how this works is my oldest son, Forrest, paying bills when he was six years old. At that time, we lived in a little three-stoplight town, about two blocks from an old-fashioned courthouse square. On a one-mile walk, we could go to the library, pay the electric bill, stop by the bank, and visit the post office. The first time Forrest went into each place, I went with him, introduced him to the clerks, and explained that we were homeschooling. After that, I would wait on the sidewalk with Andrew and Perry in the stroller while Forrest went inside alone to take care of business. The "Look what I did!" expression on his face when he would walk out of the electric company with a receipt, or the post office with a book of stamps, was precious. He still remembers that time with great pleasure.

> Your children need to gain a good work ethic and an attitude of gratefulness that can be achieved first and foremost by their involvement with the daily care of the family and home. . . . You as a mom also need to delegate many aspects of the daily home care because you are most valuable to your family as a wife and mom, and not the housekeeper.
>
> BROOK WAYNE
> from *Full-Time Parenting* by Israel Wayne

Most parents assign their children chores, but why not think bigger? You can gradually delegate the running of the entire household to your children. This may require lowering your cleanliness standards a bit, and initially it takes more work to teach the kids how to do the work than to do it yourself. But they will need to know these skills when they are adults, so you may as well teach them now.

My boys are currently twenty-one, eighteen, seventeen, and thirteen. They do all the housework and yard work and most of the cooking and laundry. (I expect to have very grateful daughters-in-law someday!) When they were in Florida with their grandparents and cousins for a week, I was reminded of just how much they take care of. To outsource everything they do, here's what I'd need to hire: a lawn care service, a launderer, a cook, a dishwasher, a janitor, a pet sitter, an errand runner, a political consultant, an intellectual sparring partner, a motivational speaker, a historian, makers of gross noises (OK, so I wouldn't hire out burping contests, but hey, they're boys!), a computer technician, a trash hauler, a firewood chopper, a book discussion group, an office assistant, a handyman, and a court jester. But no one could replace their hugs!

When my boys were younger, I assigned work to the youngest child who was capable of doing it to avoid the common pitfall of piling everything on the oldest child. I also rotated repetitive tasks so that the same person didn't get stuck with the same chore all the time. Now that they're older, they prefer to take responsibility for designated tasks so that it's always clear who should do what. For example, Andrew and Perry used to share responsibility for dishes and pet care. They initially rotated so that whoever had the harder job in one department had the easier job in the other: On the day someone cleaned the litter box, he put away clean dishes; on the day he washed dishes, he fed the cats. We later simplified this by assigning total kitchen duty and total pet duty on different days. Eventually they chose to streamline the process further by assigning all pet care to Andrew and all kitchen duty to Perry.

The sample chore charts in this chapter illustrate how I allocated housework among the boys at different stages of our family life. Sample Chore Chart 1 is a simple spreadsheet from 2007 with a section for each child and a column for each day of the week. You'll notice that in addition to chores, the chart includes reminders for the boys to read their Bibles, do their schoolwork, exercise, and drink water. This chart is similar to my Weekly Plan and Daily Tasks list. Once the boys firmly established certain habits, I removed these line items from the checklist.

I've learned to do more delegating and to let things go. It's been great to see my daughters and husband do tasks their own way, often better than I used to do them. It's made a big difference since we work as a team. I'm learning that I am not the Queen of the Universe and the weight of the entire household does not rest on my shoulders.
ELEANOR JOYCE, Pennsylvania

Sample Chore Chart 2 is an even simpler three-column Word document from 2012. Only three boys were included because Forrest was in college. He was living at home, but since he was taking a full course load and working two part-time jobs, he was exempt from most household duties except for dusting weekly and taking care of his own laundry. He also ran errands and helped drive his brothers to their various activities. This chart reflects that the boys were older and includes several outside activities such as Scouts and sports. An "As Needed" category at the bottom of each column is a convenient place to note items that don't always fall on a specific day, such as mowing and laundry.

Posting the chore chart in a public place (like on the refrigerator) helps eliminate arguments about whose turn it is to wash the dishes, mow the lawn, etc. It allows Mom not to have to repeat instructions and also to check at a glance and see what's been done.

One of my rules for both chores and homeschool assignments: If it's not checked off, it didn't happen. Or, to be a bit more accurate, if it's not checked off, it's not finished yet. If your job is to wash

Sample Chore Chart 1

FORREST (15)	S	M	T	W	R	F	S
Make bed							
Read Bible							
Sweep							
Drink water							
School assignments	x						
Run/exercise	x						
Dirty clothes in basket							
Put away clean clothes	x						
Mow/weedeat yard	x						
Clean bathrooms	x		x	x		x	x
Dust	x	x	x		x	x	x

THOMAS (7)	S	M	T	W	R	F	S
Make bed							
Read Bible							
Feed & water Jodie							
Drink water							
School assignments	x						
Run/exercise	x						
Dirty clothes in basket							
Put away clean clothes	x						
Pick up sticks for mowing	x						

ANDREW (12)	S	M	T	W	R	F	S
Make bed							
Read Bible							
Cats a.m.							
Trash/recycling				x		x	x
Drink water							
School assignments	x						
Cats p.m.							
Run/exercise	x						
Dirty clothes in basket							
Put away clean clothes	x						
Mow/weedeat our yard	x						

PERRY (11)	S	M	T	W	R	F	S
Make bed							
Read Bible							
Kitchen a.m.							
Kitchen noon							
Drink water							
School assignments	x						
Kitchen p.m.							
Run/exercise	x						
Dirty clothes in basket							
Put away clean clothes	x						
Wash/fold laundry	x						
Vacuum	x						

dishes, that job is not finished until you have hung up the wet dish towel to dry and checked "wash dishes" off your list. If your job is to take care of laundry, that job is not finished until you have put all the laundry in its appropriate closets and/or drawers, returned the empty laundry basket to the bathroom, and checked "laundry" off your list.

Children need to learn to cook as well as to do household chores. I trained my boys to be very self-sufficient so that they're capable of taking care of themselves when they need to. Once when I was going to be gone at suppertime for a meeting, a friend asked, "What are your children going to have for supper while you're gone?" I said, "Whatever they fix. The pantry is stocked, the freezer is stocked, and the refrigerator is stocked. They can cook their own supper." They often cook for themselves—or for the entire family—even when I'm at home. I once walked in on eleven-year-old Thomas instructing nineteen-year-old Forrest how to make a better omelet.

How much my boys pitch in to help was made clear in an amusing way several years ago. In a move I can attribute only to temporary insanity, I scheduled back-to-back birthday parties one Friday afternoon. Thomas's seventh birthday party was from 1:00 to 3:00 to make it convenient for the other moms in our homeschool co-op. (Co-op students in K–2 finish at 1:00, but the older students stay until 3:00.) Perry's eleventh birthday party began at 3:00. I

Sample Chore Chart 2

ANDREW (17)

SUNDAY	MONDAY	TUESDAY	WEDNESDAY
10:30 — church	4:00 — piano	Read Bible	5:30 — church
Read Bible	6:00 — Scouts	Litter boxes	Read Bible
Litter boxes	Read Bible	Feed/water cats	Litter boxes
Feed/water cats	Bring in trash can	Schoolwork	Feed/water cats
Take out trash	Litter boxes		Take out trash
	Feed/water cats		Schoolwork
	Schoolwork		

THURSDAY	FRIDAY	SATURDAY	AS NEEDED
Read Bible	8:00–3:00 — co-op	Read Bible	Laundry
Bring in trash can	Read Bible	Litter boxes	Mow
Litter boxes	Litter boxes	Feed/water cats	
Feed/water cats	Feed/water cats		
Schoolwork			

PERRY (16)

SUNDAY	MONDAY	TUESDAY	WEDNESDAY
10:30 — church	6:00 — Scouts	4:00 — cross-country	5:30 — church
Read Bible	Read Bible	Read Bible	Read Bible
Kitchen	Kitchen	Kitchen	Kitchen
	Clean bathrooms	Schoolwork	Schoolwork
	Schoolwork		

THURSDAY	FRIDAY	SATURDAY	AS NEEDED
4:00 — cross-country	8:00–3:00 — co-op	Read Bible	Laundry
6:00—Ultimate Frisbee	Read Bible	Kitchen	Clean for PopPop
Read Bible	Kitchen		
Kitchen	Schoolwork		
Clean bathrooms			
Schoolwork			

THOMAS (12)

SUNDAY	MONDAY	TUESDAY	WEDNESDAY
10:30 — church	6:00 — Scouts	Read Bible	5:30 — church
Read Bible	Read Bible	Feed/water dog	Read Bible
Feed/water dog	Feed/water dog	Sweep	Feed/water dog
Sweep	Sweep	Empty dishwasher	Sweep
Empty dishwasher	Empty dishwasher	Schoolwork	Empty dishwasher
	Schoolwork		Schoolwork

THURSDAY	FRIDAY	SATURDAY	AS NEEDED
6:00—Ultimate Frisbee	8:00–3:00 — co-op	Read Bible	Laundry
Read Bible	Read Bible	Feed/water dog	Pick up sticks for mowing
Feed/water dog	Feed/water dog	Sweep	
Sweep	Sweep	Empty dishwasher	
Empty dishwasher	Empty dishwasher		
Schoolwork			

forgot that Forrest, Andrew, and Perry—my right-hand men—would still be in class during Thomas's party. I had already sent the invitations and everybody had already accepted, so I thought, "Surely I can handle six little boys for two hours on my own." Right!

We didn't have any serious issues, but it was stressful running around to prevent potential disasters without any backup. It was challenging to keep all the boys in the same general area—upstairs or down, inside or out—because I couldn't be in two places at the same time to supervise their ongoing reenactment of every battle known to history using swords, Nerf guns, lightsabers, and Civil War-style wooden muskets.

I'm used to delegating crowd control and battle supervision to my lieutenants, but they were in logic class and music class. The moms picked up their kids around 3:00 just as Perry's friends arrived for his party. The eleven-year-old bunch was much more self-sufficient, and Forrest and Andrew were home by then to help. I sat down to rest for a few minutes and actually dozed off on the couch even though full-volume activity was going on all around me.

When I regained consciousness and sanity, I was reminded of what a tremendous blessing my four boys are. At that time we had been on our own for nearly six years (thirteen now), and they have become so responsible and independent. This is a huge contribution to my ability to work from home and continue homeschooling as a single mom. I am truly blessed.

Teach Your Children Independence

If you have an infant, you simply will not be able to accomplish the same things you will when your kids are older, unless you have help. And that's OK. We all have different priorities in different seasons of life. As your children grow older, teaching them to be independent is an extension of teaching them to be responsible.

You will have to be very hands-on at first as you train them to accomplish a particular task. As they become competent at the task, turn it over to them more and more. Once they master it, they can tackle the chore independently. For example, if you're teaching a child how to wash dishes, begin by explaining while you demonstrate. Next, coach him step by step as he washes his first dish, and then a whole sink full of dishes. Gradually shift to supervising quietly and answering questions. Finally, when your child has successfully washed the dishes several times without coaching or questions, he has mastered the task and should be able to do it without supervision or reminders. A chore chart can help keep him on track, but ultimately the chore should become a habit.

Some moms are initially uncomfortable with the idea of their children's independence, especially if they're used to peppering the kids with reminders and hovering over them. How can you make sure they are doing what they are supposed to do if you let them be independent? The solution is simple: Inspect what you expect. That's how you add accountability to independence. I have sometimes gone too long without inspecting and eventually discovered that not everything got done. Inspecting regularly (daily for younger children) keeps them from falling behind and holds them accountable.

> The mother who takes pains to endow her children with good habits secures for herself smooth and easy days; while she who lets their habits take care of themselves has a weary life of endless friction with the children.
> CHARLOTTE MASON
> *Home Education*

When my boys were younger, I learned that if their bedroom door remained closed, it usually indicated the presence of a catastrophe inside—some mountainous combination of toys and laundry. The more responsible and independent your children become, the less supervision and inspection they should need.

I didn't advocate independence when my oldest son was young because I didn't think he could do anything. In my eyes, he was a helpless little child who needed his mommy to do everything for him. Over the years, as I had more children, I wised up a bit, and Forrest eventually earned the nickname "Mr. Responsible."

Older children can also help train younger children to do household tasks. When my youngest son was five, I walked into the kitchen and found him using the microwave. "Um, Thomas, what are you doing?" I inquired. He replied, "Cooking waffles," as if it were the most ordinary thing in the world. "What do you mean you're cooking waffles?" He looked at me in disbelief and said, "Perry taught me how to use the microwave." The nine-year-old had taught the five-year-old how to microwave frozen waffles because he was tired of doing it *for* him. And now the five-year-old was perfectly capable of doing it himself. A few months later I found Andrew, age eleven, teaching Perry how to use the dishwasher because he was tired of being the only one who knew how to run it. (Note to self: Have Perry teach Thomas how to use the washer and dryer!)

Children can usually do a lot more than we think they can do. Keep safety in mind and make their duties age-appropriate. Then set high expectations and watch them live up to them!

Teach Your Children Initiative

Taking initiative goes a step beyond being responsible and independent; it's noticing something that needs to be done that's not your normal responsibility and taking care of it yourself. Once, we made *initiative* the word of the week in our home. We talked frequently about taking initiative and doing things on your own initiative. For the next few months, the boys would come to me and excitedly report that they had done something on their own initiative, and I really praised that. The greatest efficiency is possible in the home when you're not having to micromanage because your children are doing things on their own.

The goal of routines in your children's lives is to train them to be responsible and to take initiative without being told. In other words, the more routine there is in their lives, the more they should begin to take initiative in other areas, independently and without prompting.

Clay and Sally Clarkson
Educating the WholeHearted Child

Andrew is our Mr. Fix-It. He has always been intrigued by tools and how things work. He instinctively understands how things are put together, and he learns by following around every plumber, electrician, or repairman who comes to our house. When he was twelve, I noticed him walking around with a screwdriver, a tape measure, a marker, a flashlight, and a pocketknife. I asked what he was doing, and he replied matter-of-factly, "Fixing the bathroom doorknob." That's initiative!

True confession: In our home, somehow initiative doesn't always seem to apply to stray papers or random socks on the floor. We certainly haven't achieved perfection. But my boys have continued to act more and more on their own initiative as they've gotten older.

After we had experienced such success with the word *initiative*, I introduced the term *alacrity*, meaning promptness in response or cheerful readiness. That's a great goal for all our children: to take care of things promptly and cheerfully and to be ready to meet their responsibilities.

Teach Your Children Service

The words we use are important. One of my favorite phrases is "Serve your brother." Instead of saying "Will you take this to Forrest?" I'll say, "Will you serve your brother Forrest by taking this to him?" Or I might ask, "Will you serve your brother Perry? He's not feeling well today, so would you take over his responsibility to wash the dishes?" It's amazing what a different attitude that inspires. It's not just "Ugh, more work for me to do," but it's the spiritual attitude of service and being a blessing to someone else. Try incorporating that language—"serve your father," "serve your mother," "serve your sister," "serve your brother"—into your instructions to your children.

Teach them to serve beyond the bounds of your family as well. They can rake leaves for an elderly neighbor, help you prepare and deliver a meal to a family with a new baby, volunteer with you at a local food pantry, and so on. All of my boys have done many community service projects with their Boy Scout troop, and Forrest has participated in state and international missions trips.

Remember, your own example of serving your family and others with a cheerful heart is a powerful model for your children.

> When we turn our thoughts to homeschooling, to molding the hearts of our children, this vision of Jesus as Servant provides the foundation for a biblical value system. What is more valuable: to be served or to served?
>
> MICHAEL CARD
> *The Homeschool Journey*

Take Action!

☐ How will you teach your children to be responsible?

☐ How will you teach your children to be independent?

☐ How will you teach your children to take initiative?

☐ How will you teach your children to serve?

CHAPTER 11

Making Memories

*Many times you are not choosing what to do with the two
or three hours for the immediate result, but you are choosing a memory
(or choosing not to have that memory) for a lifetime. . . . When you
choose a memory in this way, you are choosing to lose hours
of time—in order to keep them!*
EDITH SCHAEFFER, *What Is a Family?*

Family Night is a tradition in our home. No matter how busy I am
during the week, no matter what deadlines I have, my boys know
that on Family Night, I'm all theirs. We watch a movie together or
play cards or a board game. During the winter, we often enjoy a fire
in the woodstove and make s'mores. When the boys were younger,
they liked to camp out in the living room on Family Night as well.

We usually do this on a Friday or Saturday night. We've missed a week now and then, but it's a tradition we all treasure.

Ironically, when your family is together almost all the time, it can sometimes be challenging to pull away from the demands of homeschooling and home business to just enjoy being together and have fun as a family. But taking a break is good for parents and children alike.

Build Family Traditions

Family traditions are comforting and reassuring, and they help build a sense of family identity. Family Night was the first thing my boys mentioned when I asked for suggestions for this chapter. We also enjoy doughnuts for breakfast on the first day of our homeschool year and birthday dinners at restaurants chosen by the birthday boy. I give each boy at least one ornament every Christmas, and they're surprisingly sentimental about them. And in this book-loving family, they know their Christmas and birthday gifts will always include books.

> You as a homemaker essentially create original artwork. Your family has never existed before and will never exist again. Every day you paint another memory in their lives.
> DR. MARY ANN FROEHLICH
> *What's a Smart Woman Like You Doing in a Place Like This?*

Seasonal decorations are another tradition, even in a house full of boys. In the winter, we enjoy lighting candles at the dinner table, even if it's not a fancy meal. In spring and summer, we decorate the table with daffodils, azaleas, or tulips from our yard. Our autumn table decoration is a big wooden bowl full of decorative gourds. We hang seasonal wreaths on our front door year-round and drape garlands on the mantel and through the baskets on top of the bookcases.

We found some medieval-looking pewter plates at a yard sale and enjoy using them for special meals. There's absolutely nothing medieval about the menu or the decorations other than the plates, but they're a lot of fun.

Another of our family traditions is Homeschool Freedom Day. One of the things I love about homeschooling is the flexibility to set our own schedule, so I declared an official holiday to celebrate it. On the first day of public school where we live, we do not do any schoolwork, even if we've already started our school year. We take a quilt and a picnic to a local park and enjoy the trees and the breeze and the sun and the freedom. Sometimes other homeschooling families join us. One year when the weather was even hotter than usual and humidity was at 93 percent, the park just wasn't appealing, so we stayed there only a little while and enjoyed lunch in the air-conditioned comfort of our favorite Mexican restaurant. Try celebrating your own Homeschool Freedom Day!

> There is something about saying, "We *always* do this," which helps to keep the years together. Time is such an elusive thing that if we keep on meaning to do something interesting but never doing it, year would follow year with no special thoughtfulness being expressed in making gifts, surprises, charming table settings, and familiar, favorite food.
>
> EDITH SCHAEFFER
> *What Is a Family?*

Spend One-on-One Time with Each Child

If you have more than one child, you know how hard it can be to spend quality one-on-one time with each of them. The more children you have, the harder it becomes, but it's well worth the effort.

Individual instruction time is a natural part of homeschooling, but make sure you spend some time with each child that's not focused on academics. They all need time just to hang out with you and to share their hearts without the risk of a sibling overhearing or interrupting. You can accomplish this at home by sending the other children outside while you and one child talk indoors. Or you can take one child into your office, study, or bedroom while the others play, study, or work elsewhere in the house.

Leaving the house makes time together a special treat. If your husband, grandparents, friend, or babysitter can take care of the other children for a while, taking one child with you away from the home provides a great opportunity for extended conversation.

Try taking only one child with you while you run errands. I used to value my errand time primarily as time alone, and I still do sometimes. However, I've found that taking one of the boys along can be fun and rewarding for me as well as for them. We have time to talk, and they learn a lot by helping me at our various destinations. All of my boys know how to choose groceries, compare prices, estimate the total cost of our purchase, load and unload a shopping cart without squishing bread, bag groceries, and ask a salesperson for information or assistance.

Taking a child out for a meal or a snack can be a special reward for an accomplishment, part of a birthday celebration, or just a way to make her feel special. This is an especially good way to get reticent children to open up. Three of my boys are very talkative, but Andrew is usually quiet and reserved. I recently took him to Starbucks for a salted caramel hot chocolate (heavenly!) to thank him for helping me with several projects. I didn't have an agenda for our conversation, but eventually he began to tell me what was on his mind, including college and career options. It was a delight for me to hear him share his heart.

If you travel for business, consider taking one child along

with you sometimes, especially if there's a connection between your trip and one of his talents or special interests. Forrest was very interested in business from around age eleven, so I took him to several conferences for entrepreneurs. With a little prompting, he introduced himself to the speakers, and that quickly became a tradition. At one event he even took a speaker to dinner. Forrest made all the arrangements himself and asked the hotel concierge to recommend a good restaurant nearby.

Andrew likes science, math, and nature. I've already mentioned our trip to the Grand Canyon when he was ten. When I asked him "What was your favorite part about this trip?" he replied, "My favorite part was sitting on the front porch of our cabin with you, looking at the stars." That's one of my most treasured memories, and it taught me an important lesson. It wasn't necessarily the grand things we were doing, but it was the time with me that meant the most to him. That inspired me to begin taking the boys with me one at a time on local errands more often.

> The ability to demonstrate true love by listening is one of the greatest pluses of a homeschool education.
> MICHAEL CARD
> *The Homeschool Journey*

Perry loved to draw when he was younger, and I started dreaming about taking him to the Louvre someday. Just a week after I set that goal, I learned about a huge exhibit from the Louvre at the High Museum in Atlanta, only six hours from our home in Mississippi. (A little closer than Paris!) I loved seeing the art, but even better was watching Perry soak it all in. He spent an hour copying a still life by Renoir and another hour copying Raphael's portrait of Baldassare Castiglione. On our way out, one of the guards told me that drawing was prohibited in the exhibit, but they had let Perry continue because he was so absorbed in his work. I still hope to take him to Paris someday, but we did what we could at the time instead of waiting for someday to see art from the Louvre.

At age eleven, Thomas had never seen the ocean, so when my mastermind team scheduled a business retreat on the Florida coast, I knew he had to come along. I'll never forget watching him take in the Atlantic for the first time! Orlando just happens to be on the way from Mississippi to Vero Beach, so we made a little detour to Disney World, which his brothers had already visited. As the youngest of four, he has always had competition for my time and attention, so we both relished the extended one-on-one time together.

> Being available for my family brings me the greatest satisfaction in my daily life. Putting family time appointments on the calendar ensures that the important time with family isn't put off for a "better time" that never comes. Plus, since it's on the calendar, we are free to enjoy ourselves. There's no small voice badgering me to "get on with real work." My husband and I finally took a day trip to a place we've wanted to see for years. We put it on the calendar, arranged to be off from work, and had a wonderful day! Now we can't figure out why we waited so long.
> CATHY SPAIN, Texas

Explore the World

If your budget permits, a family vacation is a great way to build memories. I have many fond remembrances of family trips from my own childhood. When I was married, we enjoyed many trips to my in-laws' condo in Destin. I loved Disney World as a child and hoped to take my boys someday. When my friend Rhea Perry scheduled a home business conference in Orlando, it was a great opportunity to meet that goal, and my generous parents helped pay for our trip. Thomas was too young to enjoy Disney World, so he stayed behind with his dad and grandparents. The other boys and I got more adventure than we bargained for when Hurricane Jeanne hit Florida during the trip, but Disney World was open the very next day. (Shortest lines ever!) I was so thankful that God provided us with this memorable opportunity.

> The world is a book, and those who do not travel read only one page.
> AUGUSTINE OF HIPPO

When you travel to a new place, doing some research ahead of time can make all the difference. In addition to finding information online, buying a travel guidebook is a wise investment. If you're spending hundreds or even thousands of dollars on a trip, isn't it worth twenty dollars to help you get the most out of it? You don't have to preschedule every hour or even every day, but a good guidebook can help you find great hotels and restaurants and inform you about must-see places you might otherwise miss.

Even if a vacation isn't feasible, don't let budget limitations keep you from having fun as a family. Check the newspaper and ask friends for suggestions of easy, simple, inexpensive, or even free things to do locally. The main thing is spending fun time together. Our town has free family movie nights outdoors downtown in good weather. Keep an eye out for inexpensive local concerts or plays. Going to the park is always fun and makes a nice break from your own backyard. When we lived in another town, we enjoyed spending the day at a nearby lake. The boys would throw a ball while I read, and we'd enjoy a picnic and a walk in the woods together. We had a wonderful time, and it didn't cost us a dime.

Spend time with your extended family as well. My parents were so faithful about taking my sister and me to see our grandmother at least once a year, even though it was a sixteen-hour drive. I have many precious memories of those visits. Treasure the time you and your children have with grandparents and great-grandparents—you never know how long you will have them. My parents moved to our town two years before my mom's death, and I am so thankful for the extra time my boys and I were able to spend with her. My dad still lives about three miles from us, and we are blessed to see him often. My boys enjoy visiting their father's family as well and have lots of fun with their eight cousins. If your extended family lives far away, you'll have to make an extra effort, but the time together is worth it.

Enjoy the Journey as Well as the Destination

Have you ever been so focused on your agenda that you've completely missed unique opportunities along the way? A few years ago, world-famous musician Joshua Bell played his Stradivarius violin incognito in a Metro station in Washington, D.C. Video footage from a hidden camera shows that most passersby were oblivious to the beautiful music.[1] What are you missing by not paying attention?

Learn to enjoy the journey as well as the destination. During my childhood, my family often drove on the beautiful Natchez Trace to visit my grandmother. Our usual rest stop had a marker indicating a scenic lookout point, but never once did we take time to drive the winding one-mile road to the top of the hill. Once when stopping there as an adult, I decided to see what I'd been missing. There was a gorgeous view for miles above the verdant treetops. All those years I'd missed it! Every time I pass there now, I make sure to allow at least fifteen or twenty minutes to go to the top of the hill, walk around to stretch my legs, and just soak in the beautiful view.

After that experience changed my mindset, I began looking for other ways to enjoy the journey. When Perry and I were traveling to Nashville for a conference when he was ten, we stopped at another rest stop on the Natchez Trace. I was in a hurry to get to Nashville so we would have plenty of time to see the life-size replica of the Parthenon, but Perry—who has loved to climb since before he could walk—spotted some big rocks beyond the parking lot. He begged, "Oh, Mom, please! I was born to climb! Let me climb these rocks." He climbed for half an hour while I walked around, and we were both refreshed. Just before we left, another traveler told us about a waterfall just two miles up the road, so we decided to check it out. It was a mile past our exit, and we would never have known about it if we hadn't lingered at the rocks. The waterfall was beautiful, and Perry was amazed that I let him climb down the steep trail and stick his feet in the water. I had so much fun watching him—he looked just like Huckleberry Finn.

> "It's a dangerous business, Frodo, going out of your door. You step into the Road, and if you don't keep your feet, there's no knowing where you might be swept off to."
> BILBO BAGGINS in J. R. R. Tolkien's *The Fellowship of the Ring*

Being productive and efficient is wise, but don't be so focused on the clock that you miss the delightful serendipity of discovery.

Preserve Family Memories for the Future

Finding time to make memories can be challenging, and documenting them can be even more so—but it's well worth the effort. You may think you'll never forget your children's cute sayings and habits and special family times, but as your brain gets more and more crowded—and, let's face it, older—the memories will start to slip away despite your best intentions. Unless you write them down now.

As a new mom, I was determined to do everything "right." I

marked every milestone in an adorable Peter Rabbit baby calendar. When my second son was born, I was too frazzled to find my good pen and use my best handwriting, so I developed an alternative that I call microwave journaling. I kept a legal pad and a pen on top of the microwave. Every time one of the boys lost a tooth, took a first step, or said or did something cute, I hastily scrawled it and the date on the pad. Later on, when I got around to working on baby books and scrapbooks, I used those notes to fill in memorable details. (I might be a little obsessive: In the interim, I typed the notes to make them more legible and easier to search.) Decide what works for you. Microwave journaling is handy because the pad is right there in the kitchen, and it takes away the pressure to write beautifully on the spur of the moment.

> The palest ink is clearer than the fondest memory.
> CHINESE PROVERB

Take photographs—lots of them. I took about three hundred photos of the first month of my first baby's life, and that was in the days before digital cameras and iPhones. The other boys were not documented in quite such extreme detail, but I made sure to take plenty of pictures of them as well. It's an old joke—but too often true—that our youngest children have no baby books. At least take the pictures, even if you wait until later to put them in books.

Most people take pictures of baby milestones, birthdays, Christmas, vacations, graduations, weddings, and other special events, but don't forget to photograph ordinary moments and places. I take pictures of my boys with their pets, playing with favorite toys, reading favorite books, or just hanging out on ordinary days. I also take pictures of their rooms—and every room in the house—as well as outdoor shots of the house and yard. I have fond memories of some of my childhood homes, but almost no exterior pictures. I would love to have a picture of my grandmother's house, but I don't, and it has been torn down. I can see it in my mind, but I can't share it with my children. When each of my boys was born, I walked through our entire house and yard with a video camera in addition to taking snapshots.

You probably take pictures when you travel, but do you think to collect the details that tell the stories? Pick up brochures, take notes on what you learn from tour guides, and take close-up photos of signs and scenic markers. You may not put those sign photos in an album, but taking a photo is quicker than writing down the details you want to remember.

Keep backups of your digital photos, and print them out and put them in albums when you can. If you have photos from a film camera, keep the negatives in a safe place, separate from the prints. Keep a few special pictures in a safe deposit box. Make sure your albums and supplies are acid-free and lignin-free to protect your photos.

The ideal is to stay current with putting photos in albums as you take them. This keeps them safe, helps you document your memories while they are fresh, and makes it easy for the family to reminisce together. The reality, however, is that documentation of life events is not always a top priority in a busy household. In case you're wondering, no, my own albums aren't anywhere close to current. I'll work on them again someday, probably when I have an empty nest.

> Every child's mind is a curator of memories.
> KATHY PEEL
> *The Busy Mom's Guide to a Happy, Organized Home*

If you have an overwhelming backlog of photos, start with recent ones and try to stay current going forward. Tackle the older ones later when you have more time. If, like me, you have inherited boxes of old family photos, start by categorizing them by decade or year and make notes to help you organize them. Ask relatives to help you identify people and places and share stories about what's in the photos.

Interview older family members while you can. They have so much history and wisdom to share. I interviewed my grandmother and great-aunt on video, and they talked not only about family stories (like my grandfather picking out my grandmother as his future wife when she was just an infant), but also about what it was like to live through the Great Depression. I regret that I didn't do the same with my mom—it never occurred to me she would die in her early seventies. Interview your children on video from time to time as well to capture their current speech, personalities, and mannerisms as well as their appearance at different ages.

Despite all these admonitions to document life with plenty of photographs, don't be so focused on the camera lens that you miss out on what's happening around you.

As with the rest of this book, your family traditions and recordkeeping may be quite different from mine because each family is different. Find what works for you as you seek to make meaningful memories together.

Take Action!

☐ What traditions are important to your family? Are you diligent to maintain those traditions? Would you like to start a new tradition?

☐ Make a plan for spending special one-on-one time with each of your children this week.

☐ Where would you like to travel as a family? How will you make it happen?

❑ How are you staying connected with your extended family? What can you do to improve in this area?

❑ What are some simple, inexpensive, local things you can do to have fun as a family?

❑ Have you learned to enjoy the journey as well as the destination? If not, what will you do to be alert to opportunities along the way?

❑ How are you preserving your family memories? Develop a safe storage system for your photographs and memorabilia. Interview older family members while you can.

CHAPTER 12

Managing Your Home

*She looks well to the ways of her household, and does
not eat the bread of idleness.*
PROVERBS 31:27

Training your children, making family memories, and managing
your home are important activities that have an impact far beyond
your own front door.

Homeschooling moms understand this well, but the busyness
of life can sometimes be overwhelming and tempt us to forget the
profound significance of our work. Chores and the daily duties of
maintaining a household are among moms' biggest frustrations
and family challenges. Yet these things can also bring the greatest
satisfaction. One mom told me, "What brings me the greatest

satisfaction is having a clean home with a well-maintained schedule." Another said she feels satisfied when she's had a productive day of homeschooling, prepared three healthy meals, and gotten enough work done.

However, many more moms feel burdened by the challenges of running a home. I appreciated one mom's transparency in sharing her struggles: "I really have problems getting motivated for my at-home duties. I love to go and explore and experience with my kids, and I get so overwhelmed and underenthused about what I have to do at home that I often accomplish less in a full day than I do in a day where I try to get as much as possible done by noon so we can go somewhere."

> Most of the grand-glorious headline-making events through the ages have been little more than backdrops to the real drama of green grocers, village cobblers, next-door neighbors, and grandfathers. Despite all the hype, hoopla, and hysteria of sensational turns-of-events, the ordinary people who tend their gardens and raise their children and perfect their trades and mind their businesses are the ones who make or break a culture. Just as they always have. Just as they always will.
>
> GEORGE GRANT
> *The Micah Mandate*

Housekeeping with a Grateful Heart

Whether you find them rewarding or burdensome, tasks like feeding your family, cleaning the house, and doing the laundry are necessary. As with so many things, our attitude toward these tasks makes all the difference. Brother Lawrence wrote about being as close to God in the kitchen as he was in prayer:

Lord of all pots and pans and things . . .
Make me a saint by getting meals
And washing up the plates![1]

We can honor God in the comparatively—or seemingly—small things by viewing them as willing service done for His glory. Being thankful for our blessings makes a huge difference. Many years ago an article by Gigi Graham Tchividjian, daughter of Billy and Ruth Graham, made this point so powerfully that I still keep it posted inside my pantry as a reminder. She and her family were living in the Middle East without modern conveniences such as a washer and dryer. She boiled her baby's diapers in a large pot on the stove, and she washed her other laundry in the bathtub. Her mother wrote to express her concern but added, "I am so thankful that you have clothes to wash and hands and soap with which to wash them."[2]

Let's face it, the necessity of taking care of your home is an irreducible fact. How you accomplish those tasks, though, is a matter of preference, priority, and choice.

The first option is to lower your standards. You may find this idea uncomfortable, but family relationships are more important than an immaculate house. I just have too many other commitments to do all of the daily, weekly, monthly, quarterly, and yearly tasks recommended in some homemaking books! My house might not pass the white glove test, but it's clean enough, sanitary enough, and orderly enough, and I can live with that.

A second approach we've already discussed is multitasking while you are doing basic household chores. Review phonics, math facts, or spelling with a child while cooking dinner. Fold laundry while talking on the phone, watching an educational video, or listening to an inspirational podcast.

Other options include delegating housework to your children and outsourcing it to hired help. Outsourcing is an especially useful option if you have a home business. Compare the hourly value of the time you spend on business to the hourly cost of hiring household help. You may discover that you come out ahead in terms of both money and time by paying for a cleaning service. You'll also be blessing someone else who needs the work.

> Because I'm now saying no to taking on too many outside activities, our home is organized and clean. Everyone is happier. My son said to me yesterday, "I love having a clean house."
> RITA JOHNSON, Illinois

Make Peace with Your Own Homemaking Style

One precious single mom shared her heart in response to my question about her frustrations:

> More than anything, I want to be a good homemaker. It bothers me that I cannot pour my heart into that. However, I'm extremely thankful to be able to work from home and stay with my children. I also love my work, but it's just difficult to manage good homemaking and website design with homeschooling.

It's definitely a tough challenge. Wanting to be a good homemaker is a worthy, biblical goal. But it's important not to get caught up in false guilt from the burden of trying to meet other people's standards. Being a good homemaker doesn't mean doing everything just the way you read in a book.

If you're feeling guilty for not living up to someone else's standards, consider the uniqueness of your circumstances. Who wrote the books about homemaking? Are they homeschooling? Are they running home businesses? Are they single moms? Do they have as many children as you do? Do they struggle with chronic illness? Are their recommendations appropriate for your family?

Consider what it really means for you to be a good homemaker with your own irreducible facts, and find peace in the space between the ideal and reality.

> One of our neighbors used to say that the only advantage in not being too good a housekeeper is that your guests are so pleased to feel how very much better they are.
> ELEANOR ROOSEVELT

A Place for Everything and Everything in Its Place

Cleaning and organizing your home is much more difficult when you have too many possessions. Many of the moms I talk with express their frustration in this area, saying things like "I'm drowning in stuff" or "We can't find our things." One coaching client who shared some of her challenges in managing her time sent me a list of what she called "time vampires"—fully half the items on her list had to do with possessions.

This is the single most important rule for dealing with your stuff: A place for everything and everything in its place. This helps you avoid wasting a lot of time searching for things when they're not where they should be.

Designate specific homes for all your stuff, including these items:

- Purse

- Keys

- Cell phone

- Mail

- Shoes

- Clothing

- Books

- School supplies

- Art and craft supplies

- Photographs and memorabilia

- Sports equipment

- Toys

- Music, movies, and games

- Important papers

- Pet supplies

- Cleaning supplies

- Tools

Clothes, for example, should be on your body, in a laundry basket, in the washer or dryer, on the clothesline, in a basket to be folded—or better yet, folded as soon as they come out of the dryer—or in the appropriate closet or drawer. This means there shouldn't be dirty socks (or clean ones, for that matter) scattered around the family room. (Can you tell I have four boys?) No one should have to hunt for the right shoes when the rest of the family is ready to leave for church.

Each child should have a shelf, basket, or other storage area for schoolbooks, notebooks, and supplies so no learning time will be wasted searching for a missing math book. (It must be around here *some*where!) Keep pens and pencils available in every room. If you have the space, provide an area where projects in progress (such as jigsaw puzzles, art, or Lego creations) can be left out for the family's ongoing work and enjoyment.

Train your children early to take care of their own stuff and to put everything away in its proper place.

Organize Your Papers

Even in this increasingly digital world, a big category of stuff for most families is paper. There are newsletters, sports schedules, co-op phone lists, school assignments, papers to grade, graded papers to file, newspaper clippings, magazine articles to read later or save for future research, and so much more.

> Let us view our organization systems as tools to help our families, not see our families as enemies of our organization systems.
> DR. MARY ANN FROEHLICH
> *What's a Smart Woman Like You Doing in a Place Like This?*

There are two primary ways to deal with paper: Pile it or file it. Like many other visual people, I like having important papers out where I can see them, but that growing pile quickly becomes time-wasting clutter. Keep a few important papers visible (your Monthly Calendar, Weekly Plan, Daily Tasks, etc.) and file the rest. If you write all your tasks and appointments on your weekly or daily list, you won't need a pile of papers to remind you what to do.

Your binder for your seven planning tools is also a good place to store information about upcoming activities, flyers about concerts you want to attend, schedules for music lessons, and so on. You may want to keep homeschool lesson plans in the same binder, or you may prefer to keep them in a separate binder. Whatever works best for you is fine.

I recommend keeping a printed back-up of important contact information. I use a separate slim binder for our personal phone and address book and keep it in a kitchen drawer for handy reference. I print out a paper copy of my Outlook contacts every year when I address Christmas cards and place the list in my phone binder. I also store emergency phone numbers and church and homeschool group phone and mailing lists there. This may seem excessive to younger moms who swear by their cell phones, but phones can easily be lost or stolen. They can also crash or be stepped on. How often have you seen pleas on Facebook for someone's friends to send their numbers because their phone crashed and all their contacts were lost? This has happened to my oldest son more than once. Many options are available online for digital storage and back-up, but I'm still a firm believer in the value of paper.

> I love the high-tech / high-touch dance of handwriting notes and then assimilating and processing them into the computer. I often coach people who are looking for the perfect way to use only one or the other—all paper or all computer. I've found that doing both increases the use and value of both.
> DAVID ALLEN
> *Ready for Anything*

Buy a file box or filing cabinet and set up files for all of your papers. Helpful categories might include the following:

- Finances

- Tax records

- Home inventory with photos

- Loan and mortgage paperwork

- Medical records

- Homeschool lesson plans and records

- Home business

- Family information

- Wills

- Copies of résumés, transcripts, diplomas

- Instruction manuals and warranties for equipment and appliances

- Topics that interest you (especially if you're a writer, researcher, or activist)

Hanging file folders work much better than manila folders that tend to fall over when the drawer isn't full.

To make your papers portable, use two-pocket folders. (They can go in your filing system later.) Stock up at fall back-to-school sales when office supply stories sell them for a penny. I use these when I want to take an editing project to the library or to work on while waiting for a doctor's appointment. When I travel, I often take several of these colorful folders for different projects in progress, as well as information about my trip.

Small storage boxes with separate lids are a great way to store larger projects in progress. As an editor, I'm often working on several manuscripts. I keep each manuscript in a storage box on my desk or on top of my filing cabinet for quick access.

If all this talk of paper drives you crazy, check out online resources like Cozi or Evernote. I still prefer paper, but I'm experimenting with Cozi and Evernote because I hear such good things about them.

"Edit" Your Stuff

The best way to stay in control of your stuff is to "edit" it. When I edit a manuscript, I add some things, rearrange some, and delete others. The same strategies can apply to stuff.

Here's a decision-making process you can use when you are trying to edit your stuff.

The two basic categories are (1) keep it or (2) get rid of it.

If you keep it, you have to store it. Designate a place for it. Maybe you need to add some storage boxes, bookcases, or filing cabinets. If you can't create a place for it, you shouldn't keep it.

If you haven't used it or worn it in a year, you can probably get rid of it. If you are going to get rid of it, you can sell it, give it away, or throw it away.

If you are going to sell it, you can have a yard sale, sell it on eBay, or take it to a consignment shop.

If you are going to give it away, you can share it with families in your church, neighborhood, or homeschool group or donate it to a charity.

If it's not in a good enough condition to sell or give away, throw it away and don't look back. Get rid of that burden of stuff that is not useful to anyone anymore but is just occupying space in your house and in your mind.

I experienced the power of editing my stuff several years ago. I used to shop a lot at yard sales to collect things I thought I was going to sell on eBay—someday. Finally, I realized that eBay was just not a part of my business plan, so all those boxes of stuff were just a burden. I'd spent money on these things, but I wasn't going to sell them on eBay, and I didn't have time to hold a yard sale. (Or I should say, I wasn't willing to make time for a yard sale.)

When Hurricane Katrina hit, a lot of refugees from the coast traveled north, and there was a huge relief effort here in Tupelo, Mississippi. I donated all of my "eBay inventory," including nice clothes, books, toys, games, home furnishings, kitchen supplies, linens, and more. It was such a relief to get rid of all those boxes and to be able to bless hurting people with things they desperately needed.

Meals

Like housekeeping, cooking is a delight for some moms and a burden to others. We've already talked about this in chapter 9, but we'll explore a few more strategies here.

Slow cookers are a busy mom's best friend. You can start supper in the morning while your energy is high and then enjoy a hot meal in the evening. They're also a great way to avoid heating up the kitchen with the oven on a sweltering summer day.

Cook once, eat twice. When I'm cooking supper, I always make enough so that we can have leftovers for lunch or supper the next day.

Many moms are fans of once-a-month cooking. I haven't done that on a large scale, but I buy large quantities of ground beef when it goes on sale, brown it all, use some for tacos for supper, and freeze the rest so it will be handy to add to recipes later. You can stock your freezer gradually by cooking two casseroles at a time and making double batches of soup or muffins—eat some and freeze some.

> Show hospitality to one another without grumbling.
> 1 PETER 4:9 (ESV)

Teaching your children to cook is a tremendous help and a great investment of your time. As I mentioned earlier, all of my boys know how to cook for themselves and for the family. This frees some of my time for other tasks and helps them develop an important life skill.

Use a preprinted grocery list or create your own custom list. When you open the last package of some item, add it to the list.

Using a printed list helps you remember essentials and makes it easier for everyone in the household to update the list. Keeping track of typical prices for common items helps you know when sales are good enough to stock up.

As often as possible, eat meals as a family—especially supper. Sometimes I was very slack about this when life got crazy, and I regret that. As my boys are getting older and starting to head off to college, I cherish our time together even more. Enjoy relaxed conversation rather than rushing through the meal. Ignore any ringing phone, and keep cell phones away from the table so no one is tempted to text. Focus on the people who are present at the table.

> Don't let complicated recipes and menus limit the time your family can sit around the dinner table and talk about the day. It's more important to eat together than to serve elaborate meals.
>
> KATHY PEEL
> *The Busy Mom's Guide to a Happy, Organized Home*

Sharing a meal with friends is a great way to enjoy godly fellowship. The home is a place of service as well as a refuge for the family. Thinking in terms of hospitality rather than entertaining removes the pressure to perform and helps you serve from a mindset of ministry.

Take Action!

☐ Is housekeeping a joy or a struggle for you? Do you need to change your attitude? Lower your standards? Multitask? Delegate or outsource some of your housework?

☐ Make peace with your own homemaking style. Release yourself from the burden of trying to live up to someone else's standards.

☐ Designate a place for everything, and then train yourself and your family to keep everything in its place.

☐ Organize your important papers or explore online resources to store important information.

☐ Edit your stuff.

☐ Experiment with new cooking strategies.

☐ Make hospitality a priority. Invite someone to join your family for a meal this week.

CHAPTER 13

All of Life Is Learning

And these words that I command you today shall be on your heart. You shall teach them diligently to your children, and shall talk of them when you sit in your house, and when you walk by the way, and when you lie down, and when you rise.
DEUTERONOMY 6:6–7, ESV

Is it "school" when my thirteen-year-old goes on a mission trip to Peru or attends an Internet marketing conference with me? Is it school when he reads a book about ancient Greece just for the fun of it or earns his swimming merit badge at Boy Scout camp? Is it school when my ten-year-old interrupts watering his sunflower garden to examine an interesting insect and runs inside for his beloved field guide so he can identify it? Is it school when my nine-year-old discovers a new drawing technique by trial and error or asks an interesting theological question out of the blue? Is it school when my five-year-old snuggles in my lap for a story and later acts out the plot with his stuffed animals? Each of these is a powerful example of learning based on genuine curiosity and interest and is just as important to a child's education as formal lessons.

> Your role as a home-educating parent, then, is to provide a rich and lively living and learning environment in which your children can exercise their God-given drive to learn and then to biblically train and instruct your children within the natural context of your home and family life. It's that simple.
> CLAY AND SALLY CLARKSON
> *Educating the WholeHearted Child*

This chapter is by no means a comprehensive guide to homeschooling. Rather, it is a collection of some of the best strategies I've learned during seventeen years of educating my children at home. You can find much more detailed information in my favorite books about homeschooling. These are listed in appendix A.

Why Should You Homeschool?

What are your reasons for homeschooling? Whether you're just getting started or you're a veteran homeschooler, a reminder of the many benefits can help renew your vision for why you're doing what you're doing and can encourage you to stay the course when the going gets tough.

Here's a quick look at some of the advantages of homeschooling:

- Being the primary influence in your children's lives

- Discipling them in the faith

- Having quality and quantity time together

- Building stronger parent-child bonds and sibling relationships

- Sharing all of life together instead of fragmenting the family

- The greater efficiency of one-on-one tutoring

- Allowing your children to learn at their own pace

- The ability to pursue special interests

- Customizing your educational approach to suit your child's learning style

- Accommodating special needs

- Encouraging critical thinking

- Facilitating independent learning

- Nurturing rather than squashing creativity

- Living in the real world rather than the artificial boxes of age segregation

- Opportunities for volunteer service

Our approach to education, then, should be one that integrates the heart and mind. This embodies true understanding. Our children need to be nurtured, to be raised and trained with all areas of development taken into consideration. And this nurturing does not take place only in the preschool years. It is a continual process. Eventually, the need to be nurtured will mature into the need to be discipled and mentored. Our children need individualized attention. . . . Our children need our time if they are to grow in wisdom—that unique blending of the heart and the mind.

SUSAN CARD
The Homeschool Journey

- Avoiding educational labels

- Avoiding danger and negative peer influences

- Having more time for positive socialization

And the list goes on and on.

Does homeschooling work? Yes!

In the area of academics, home-educated students typically score fifteen to thirty percentile points higher than the norm on standardized tests, and more and more colleges are actively recruiting homeschoolers.[1] Homeschoolers do well in the workplace. Many become entrepreneurs, and the Society for Human Resource Management reports that companies who have employed homeschoolers generally praise them.[2] Homeschool parents, students, and graduates are good citizens as well. Many volunteer at a library, sing at nursing homes, help their neighbors, or foster or adopt children who need a home. Seventy-one percent of homeschool graduates participate in community service (as opposed to only 37 percent of similar-aged adults who attended public or private schools).[3]

How Should You Homeschool?

Just as there's no one right way to schedule your day, there is no one right way to homeschool. Homeschoolers today are blessed with an abundance of options. Whether you prefer fully scripted lessons or bare-bones guidelines, you can choose from an almost overwhelming variety of curriculum, resources, books, tutors, online classes, video courses, software, co-ops, and support groups. However, asking "What curriculum should we use?" is the wrong place to start. Before you select curriculum, you need to clarify your reasons for homeschooling and what you hope to accomplish, and then explore the variety of approaches to homeschooling. Only then will you have the information you need to begin choosing curriculum. You may prefer to blend multiple approaches and resources to create your own eclectic program. And if what you choose doesn't work out the way you've planned, you can always change direction next year.

Different authors categorize homeschooling approaches in a variety of ways and with different labels. I've included a brief overview of the six major types. There is some overlap among the categories. For example, some classical curricula use textbooks and workbooks, and some unit studies are delight directed. Some texts incorporate Charlotte Mason methods, such as narration, and are more akin to living books than traditional age-graded textbooks.

Each of these approaches has worked well for some families and poorly for others. A combination of the Charlotte Mason and classical methods has proven to be the best

> Education is not filling a bucket but lighting a fire.
> WILLIAM BUTLER YEATS

fit for my family. Again, the most important thing is to discover what works best for *your* family. I have not used all of these methods or resources, so listing them here does not constitute an endorsement. The examples I mention are representative, not comprehensive. I've included them to give you an idea of the wide variety of resources available.

TRADITIONAL

Highly structured, with an age-graded scope and sequence for each subject. Uses textbooks and workbooks and usually includes teacher manuals, tests, and answer keys. Typically designed for institutional schools and adapted for homeschooling. Includes video and online options. *Examples:* A Beka, Bob Jones University Press, Alpha Omega, Christian Liberty Press, Calvert School, Mott Media, Rod and Staff.

CLASSICAL

This approach has produced great minds throughout history. Follows the three stages of the trivium: grammar, logic/dialectic, and rhetoric. Emphasizes Latin, logic, eloquence in writing and speaking, and participating in the "great conversation" of classic literature. Very academic/intellectual. *Examples:* Trivium Pursuit, *The Well-Trained Mind*, Veritas Press, Memoria Press, Canon Press.

PRINCIPLE APPROACH

Emphasizes America's Christian history, living according to biblical principles, and self-government. Focuses on the four R's: research, reasoning, relating, and recording. *Examples:* James Rose, Stephen McDowell, Rosalie Slater (Foundation for American Christian Education).

CHARLOTTE MASON / LIVING BOOKS

Emphasizes short lessons, real life, nature study, and good habits. Uses "living books," which are filled with ideas to ponder rather than merely snippets of facts and are well written in an engaging, narrative style by an author who is passionate about the subject. Charlotte Mason believed that "education is an atmosphere, a discipline, a life." *Examples:* Susan Schaeffer Macaulay, Dean and Karen Andreola, Catherine Levinson, Ruth Beechick, Clay and Sally Clarkson, Charlotte Mason's *Original Home Schooling Series*, Apologia, Beautiful Feet Books, Cornerstone Curriculum, Greenleaf Press, My Father's World, Ambleside Online.

Unit Studies

A unit study integrates many subjects into a single theme or topic. Can easily be age-integrated so the entire family can learn together. Uses creative, hands-on activities and discovery learning. *Examples:* KONOS, Weaver, Valerie Bendt, Tapestry of Grace, Five in a Row, Amanda Bennett.

Unschooling, Relaxed Homeschooling, and Delight-Directed Studies

These approaches are sometimes categorized separately, but all emphasize a child's innate desire to learn, focus on the child's interests, and use a wide variety of resources and activities. Extreme unschooling uses minimal structure, instruction, and intervention, while relaxed or delight-directed homeschooling typically involves more structure. *Examples:* John Holt, John Taylor Gatto, Patrick Farenga, Mary Hood, Raymond and Dorothy Moore, Gregg Harris.

The book *Homeschooling Methods,* edited by Paul and Gena Suarez, provides a more detailed look at each approach as explained by its proponents. Home Ed Expert, an online system created by homeschooling specialists and led by curriculum expert Cathy Duffy, can help you find curricula and resources that fit your goals and teaching style, as well as your students' unique needs and learning styles.[4]

To be educated is not merely to have the ability to answer multiple-choice questions on a test. True education is a process of digestion, where knowledge becomes your own as you take information in, ponder it, grapple with it, and separate the truth from the falsehoods. If you really have knowledge, you should be able to translate it to other people. Once you can explain what you know, you are much closer to true understanding. Simple memorization is not enough. The purpose of education is not to harbor facts with our minds, but to comprehend truths. All the memorized facts come to life only as we truly understand them. And we understand them only when we become disciplined enough to ponder, to consider, to ask questions.

SUSAN CARD
The Homeschool Journey

Whatever approach or combination of approaches you choose, include a good mixture of breadth (learning a little about a lot of things) and depth (learning a lot about a few things). Make sure your children know that education is not simply checking assignments off a list. Teach them not only to answer questions but also to ask them. Encourage their curiosity and help them find the answers. "Let's go look it up" is a favorite homeschool motto. That's one reason why it's a great idea to build a home library that extends beyond this year's curriculum.

Aim to inspire a love of learning in your children. They may graduate from homeschool and perhaps from college, but their education shouldn't end there. Make it your goal to create lifelong learners. Remember, "educate" is one of the tools in the FREEDOM toolbox for grownups too!

When Should You Homeschool?

The best home education integrates school lessons with all the rest of life. Homeschooling can and should take place 24/7. That's why I consider ludicrous any state's requirements to keep "attendance" records. Nevertheless, it's important that you comply with your state and local requirements for homeschooling: Some require that your homeschool year fall within certain dates (often based on the public school calendar), and some require that you document a certain number of days per school year or hours per school day. Some require testing or notification by certain dates. Check out the daytime curfew laws in your area as well. The Home School Legal Defense Association (HSLDA) is a great place to find the laws that apply to your state.[5] As long as you comply with applicable regulations and are being diligent to educate your children, you can homeschool whenever and wherever you like.

> Education is taking place during all of the waking hours.
> SUSAN SCHAEFFER MACAULAY
> *For the Children's Sake*

You can teach on weekdays and weekends, in the daytime or nighttime. Some families choose to follow the local public school calendar, while others customize a schedule to suit their own needs. You might need to work around a home business or travel schedule, or leave some lessons until night so the kids can study with Dad. Here are just a few options:

- 9 months on, 3 months off (typical school calendar)
- 3 months on, 1 month off
- 3 weeks on, 1 week off
- 6 weeks on, 2 weeks off
- 4 days a week for 45 weeks, with 7 full weeks off

Whatever schedule or routine you follow for formal instruction, be alert for teachable moments and spontaneous opportunities. For example, I never expected to teach Business 101 in the emergency room! When Andrew was ten, he splashed some gasoline in his eye while adding fuel to the lawn mower. I got him started flushing his eye with cold water, and then called a toll-free nurse hotline. They insisted I take him to the emergency room. I could tell Andrew was going to be fine when he immediately noticed a typo the admitting nurse made. "What's 'clod water'?" he wanted to know. During our long wait for the doctor (who recommended over-the-counter eyedrops), Andrew and I chatted about business.

The topic came up when he announced, "Perry and I have decided we need to create a scam."

Hmm. "Why's that, Andrew?"

"Because we want to make money *selling people things*."

First, I explained the difference between a scam and a business. Then we discussed gross and net income, and he figured out the two ways to increase profit (increase revenue or reduce expenses). I then tried to explain the importance of having a viable market for your product. I asked, "If you want to make money selling a product, what else do you need besides something to sell?"

Over the next half hour, Andrew came up with these answers:

- A way to make the product

- Supplies to manufacture the product

- A place to sell the product

- A good product

- A fair price

- Telling people about the product

- A big sign to show how much it costs

- Making change when people give you too much money

- A cash register

Finally it clicked: "Oh, and customers," he said.

Bingo! That's the answer I was looking for.

Andrew is a nature lover, so I asked, "What if you were the only person on the planet who cared about sunflowers? What if you knew more about sunflowers than anyone else who has ever lived, and you wrote the best book about sunflowers that has ever been written? Would you make any money?"

"No," he conceded.

This concept may seem like a no-brainer, but even some adult entrepreneurs don't seem to get it.

Then we talked about selling what customers want. "What if you're selling vanilla ice cream, and not many people are buying vanilla, but everyone is asking for chocolate?" I asked.

"You start selling chocolate ice cream."

"Right! Now what if you want to mow yards, but nobody in our neighborhood wants to pay for lawn care? What if you find out what they really want is someone to wash their cars?"

"You start a car washing business." He quickly saw the value of brokering car washing by bringing customers and laborers together

> Boys and girls must have time to invent episodes, carry on adventures, live heroic lives, lay sieges and carry forts, even if the fortress be an old armchair; and in these affairs the elders must neither meddle nor make.
> CHARLOTTE MASON
> *Home and School Education*

rather than washing all the cars himself. So far, so good.

Then I threw him a curve ball. "What if you find out that in addition to car washing, people want someone to walk their dogs?" "I stay in the car-washing business because I already have everything I need for it."

Well, maybe creating multiple streams of income comes under the heading of Business 102. But I won't wait for the next ER visit.

Where Should You Homeschool?

Where can you homeschool? There's home, of course, but the possibilities are almost endless. A homeschool doesn't have to look like institutional school. Some families set aside a designated room for school, complete with old-fashioned school desks. That's fine if you have the space and it works well for you, but be careful to avoid communicating the idea that learning happens *only* in that room and only during designated hours. All of life is learning.

Children can learn indoors or outdoors, at a desk or the dining-room table, or snuggled up together on the sofa reading aloud. They can learn while perched on top of the monkey bars with a book (Andrew's favorite spot at age ten). They can learn at home, at the library, in the

> We owe it to our children to stimulate in them a wide range of interests in their elementary years. Wherever we go, whomever we talk to, whatever we see can be of some interest to children if we stand aside and let them question and consider or examine and research. It should not be "How much has our child covered?" but "How much does he care?" and "About how many things does he care?"
> KAREN ANDREOLA
> *A Charlotte Mason Companion*

car, on a field trip, or while traveling.

My boys learn when we gather under the shady pecan tree in our front yard to read from *The Swiss Family Robinson*. (I consider it a bonus when the mailman asks the thirteen-year-old, "Shouldn't you be in school today?" and he replies, "We're doing school right now.") They learn when they use their Playmobil people to reenact a history lesson. They learn when they crowd around the dining room table to make electricity with a flashlight bulb, aluminum foil, and a battery. They learn when they help me make bread. ("Why does the dough get higher, Mama?") They learn when we comparison-shop at the grocery store. They learn when we find a dead bird on the deck, look it up in a field guide, and sketch it.

Now that they're older, my boys mostly prefer to work at desks in their bedrooms upstairs, but they often hang out in the family room with their books and laptops. And we still read aloud together even though they're all perfectly capable of reading on their own.

If your homeschool is stuck in a rut, experiment with changing locations and see what develops. You may be pleasantly surprised!

Get Real with Realistic Expectations

Homeschoolers tend to be an idealistic lot, and that's a good thing. We want to aim high. But keep in mind the principle of finding peace in the space between the ideal and reality. Focus on what you *can* do rather than being paralyzed by what you can't do. Whatever your family's circumstances, whatever your kids' challenges, whatever their ages, remember to have realistic expectations for them—and for yourself.

If you have many children of different ages and abilities, your homeschool day will look very different from a day in a home with one kindergartener or one high schooler. If you or your children

I meet teaching parents all around the country and find them to be intelligent, enthusiastic, creative people doing a marvelous job of teaching their children. But sad to say, most of them do not know what a great job they are doing. Everyone thinks it goes smoothly in everyone else's house and theirs is the only place that has problems. I'll let you in on a secret about teaching: There is no place in the world where it rolls along smoothly without problems. Only in articles and books can that happen.

RUTH BEECHICK
You Can Teach Your Child Successfully

have special needs or chronic health problems, the word "realistic" takes on a whole new meaning. If you have an infant or toddler, you'll face completely different challenges from a family with all teens. The ages of your oldest and youngest children make a lot of difference. Next year's homeschool may be very different from this year's.

Come up with a realistic plan that you can actually implement rather than wasting time and energy fretting over the gaps between theory and practice, between the ideal and reality.

A Day in Our Life

We all sometimes wonder what other homeschool families' lives look like. Perhaps you'll find it encouraging to catch a real-world glimpse into one family's life (mine) instead of imagining that everyone else is managing everything perfectly all the time.

Several years ago, I participated in a blog topic called "Fly on the Wall." The instructions were: "You have to tell what your day TODAY was like—really! Not what you wish it had been like or what you'd planned for it to be like, but how it really turned out." Here's my response:

Ah, the truth, the whole truth, and nothing but the truth, eh?

Naturally, this fell on an atypical day. But as I reflect on the day, it really is representative in many ways, with independent schoolwork, attention to a variety of entrepreneurial enterprises, books, health issues, multitasking, and making the most of small bits of time.

I rose at 7:30 and read three chapters of Judges. (I'm a bit behind on Robert Murray M'Cheyne's plan for reading the Bible in a year, but I'm catching up.)

I woke Forrest and Andrew for chores and breakfast, ate my own breakfast, checked e-mail quickly, posted a blog entry, left a phone message for a publisher about an overdue book order, showered, and dressed. Perry was running a fever last night, so I let him sleep in, as well as Thomas, with whom he shares a room.

Due to ongoing back troubles, I had to go to the chiropractor this morning, about a thirty-minute drive away, so that threw a kink in our morning school routine. Fortunately, I had planned lessons a week in advance, and today was almost all independent work anyway, so I instructed Forrest and Andrew to proceed with their lessons and took Perry and Thomas with me.

Multitasking is one of my top survival strategies, so on the drive I called a friend whom I had recently counseled when she and her husband were trying to decide whether to continue homeschooling. I was delighted to learn that they will continue because "homeschooling is what we do." She's also going to be taking college classes herself. It was good to catch up with her.

While waiting at the chiropractor's office, I read F. Scott Fitzgerald's story "The Offshore Pirate" to prepare for writing about it as part of revising and expanding my book, *F. Scott Fitzgerald A to Z*, for Facts on File's new Critical

Companion series. Also while there, I ran into the friend who is coordinating our Resourcefulness and Inventions co-op this semester, and we were able to chat about plans for our meeting next week. Love that serendipity! Unfortunately, after talking with her, I realized that the "week 2" lesson plans she had e-mailed were for next week, not the week after. In my feverish fog (bronchitis wiped me out all last week), I had misunderstood the timing. So we're a little behind instead of a little ahead as I had thought. Time to revamp the lesson plans. We'll have to squeeze in a bit of extra reading tomorrow.

Got home in time to eat a quick lunch, return the publisher's phone call ("We have no record of your book order from three weeks ago!"), and return a call from a friend who wanted to know if she should buy some books in the World Explorer series. Yes, she should. (My son Forrest has an amazing collection of explorer books—that's the topic that first lit his bibliophile fire—and the Garrard World Explorer series is a major part of it. So are Ronald Syme's books, but I digress.) During my hour at home, Forrest and Andrew went across the street to mow and weed for our neighbor.

Off again to take Perry to the pediatrician, while Forrest and Andrew resumed their math, cursive, and science reading. Normally I'd wait a bit longer to see if whatever was causing Perry's fever would clear up on its own, but it's Friday (Why do kids always get sick on Friday?), and he'll be visiting his dad Sunday through Tuesday, so I didn't want to put it off. Read a chapter of Harvey and Laurie Bluedorn's wonderful book *Teaching the Trivium* during our uncharacteristically short wait at the doctor's office. Perry's ears were fine (last time it was an ear infection). His throat was red, but the strep test was negative. Diagnosis: viral pharyngitis. Give him Tylenol and let him rest.

Back home, where Perry crashed on the couch for the rest of the afternoon. Forrest finished weeding the neighbor's yard, Andrew mowed ours, and then they worked with Thomas on cleaning their rooms. Me? I took a nap. I'm not quite back up to snuff after a vicious bout with bronchitis (in July, for crying out loud!) last week, and I still run out of steam very quickly. Sure hope I don't catch what Perry has.

Squeezed in an hour or so of paperwork in my home office—paying bills, filing papers, updating lesson plans and calendar, excavating the surface of my desk. E-mailed a couple of editing clients. Made arrangements for Grandmama to keep Perry tomorrow while the rest of us visit friends who are moving to Kentucky next week. Don't want to risk sharing germs with them.

Took the easy way out and ordered pizza for supper. I didn't even feel like heating up the house to cook a frozen pizza tonight. Browsed through my Creative Memories consultant magazine during dinner. Need to order new products and alert customers about an upcoming price increase. Took a quick look at the latest issue of *Homeschooling Today* which arrived in today's mail. This will be the last issue with my name on the masthead as copy editor. I love the magazine and have enjoyed working with the good folks there, but I just have too many irons in the entrepreneurial fire.

Friday nights are family time around here—sometimes a board game, usually a video. Tonight we'll watch the second half of *The Two Towers* extended version. We love *The Lord of the Rings*—both books and movies! I'd like to think that I'll be in bed by 11:00, but it's usually midnight.

Nurture a Love of Reading

Whatever homeschooling approach you choose, I encourage you to make reading real books—not just textbooks—a priority in your family. Skill, interest, and discernment in reading have a profound effect on every other aspect of education. Reading develops the mind, builds vocabulary, provides models of good writing, expands the imagination, allows children to "travel" to new places and explore other cultures, develops empathy, and teaches by example.

Pulitzer-Prize-winning author Eudora Welty grew up in a family that valued books and reading aloud. Her childhood passion for books provides a beautiful picture of what such an environment can stimulate:

> I learned from the age of two or three that any room in our house, at any time of day, was there to read in, or to be read to. . . . It had been startling and disappointing to me to find out that story books had been written by people, that books were not natural wonders, coming up of themselves like grass. Yet regardless of where they came from, I cannot remember a time when I was not in love with them—with the books themselves, cover and binding and the paper they were printed on, with their smell and their weight and with their possession in my arms, captured and carried off to myself. Still illiterate, I was ready for them, committed to all the reading I could give them.[6]

Make reading a daily habit. Read aloud as a family and read individually. Encourage children to read books of their choice as well as assigned books. Enjoy activities such as acting out plots, drawing pictures, cooking foods mentioned in a story, or traveling to locations where favorite books are set. Visit the library and the bookstore. Make books accessible by placing bookcases throughout the house and keeping young children's books on low shelves. Set out baskets of seasonal books or books on interesting topics.

Avoid dumbed-down, poorly written books—what Charlotte Mason called "twaddle." Instead, focus on classics that are well written, contain thought-provoking ideas, and have stood the test of time. Classics include both enduring children's books by authors like Beatrix Potter and Laura Ingalls Wilder and the "great books" by authors like Charles Dickens and Jane Austen.

Choose age-appropriate books. Young children need positive examples to emulate; older students can also learn from negative examples to avoid. Ask questions about characters' choices and discuss how they could have handled things better. Use books to teach discernment. Reading books with which you disagree stretches your mind and teaches you to defend your position more skillfully.

Use living books to integrate your study of many subjects. Have your children write about what they are reading in literature, science, or history. Encourage their creativity with fun assignments such as writing their own stories, imagining alternate endings, or rewriting a passage from one author in the style of another author. For younger students, copywork and dictation incorporate vocabulary, spelling, grammar, and penmanship. Narration—having children tell you the story in their own words or explaining what they learned about a topic or character—provides early practice in composition.

> There are seasons in a child's growth that the parent must come to understand. There is the spring of lullabies and letters and the summer of simple songs, but in time the year will progress into the harvest season where the door of imagination will swing wide open to the classics of literature and great music.
>
> MICHAEL CARD
> *The Homeschool Journey*

Focus on discussion with older students. Train them to form their own opinions about what they read, and teach them to find something to appreciate about a classic even if they didn't enjoy it. Analyze how authors choose words, craft sentences, and structure arguments or plots. Encourage them to mark their books as they read. This makes the books their own, makes reading more active, and makes it easy to review. Have them keep a reading journal to record their reflections on what they read. They should focus not merely on facts but also on ideas, themes, characters, and literary style, as well as questions they want to discuss.

Building a home library helps to create a culture of reading and an atmosphere for learning. You can find great deals at secondhand bookstores, thrift shops, library sales, and yard sales. Aim for breadth (books on a wide variety of topics) and depth (many books on a specific topic). Collect fiction and nonfiction, books about your children's interests, favorite authors, and wonderful series such as the Landmark history books. Give books as birthday and Christmas gifts to build your children's personal libraries. Provide bookshelves in their rooms to hold their own collections as well as favorites from the family library.

Remember to set an example for your children. Seeing *you* reading—for pleasure as well as for learning—is a crucial part of teaching them to love books and value reading.

Teach Children of Different Ages Together

When my boys were younger, we began each day with the whole family coming together for Bible reading, prayer, Scripture memorization, poetry, and reading aloud from classic literature, followed by alternating individual work with one-on-one instruction in phonics and math. Later they would continue independent work, do chores, and enjoy free time while I worked on my business.

It makes sense to teach children of different ages together whenever possible. This is one of the advantages of homeschooling over any kind of institutional schooling, whether public, private, or parochial. Sequential skills such as math and phonics have to be taught at individual levels, of course, but most subjects can be taught to children of multiple ages at the same time.

Science, history, and literature are especially well suited to multi-level teaching. For example, instead of one child studying ancient Greece and Rome, another studying the Middle Ages, and yet another studying American history, all three can be studying the same time period. This simplifies your lesson planning and book buying, promotes family unity, and allows your children to enjoy read-alouds, projects, and field trips together as well as working independently at appropriate levels of difficulty.

When we studied early American history, for example, we were involved in a weekly co-op where the boys did hands-on activities and presented reports at a meeting each Friday. During the week,

We don't have to chart exactly what a child has "learned" from any of these sources to make it worthwhile using them. This is a different way of thinking about learning. Our job is to give the best nourishment regularly. The child takes what is appropriate to him at that time. An example is when we enjoy a book together as a family. The nine-year-old enjoys hearing J. R. R. Tolkien's *The Lord of the Rings*. He extracts nourishment for mind and spirit. The fourteen-year-old is also fed, but extracts something different. There is no "right" way to react, no list of items one has to remember. Living life isn't like that. We are individuals, and we leave it that way.
SUSAN SCHAEFFER MACAULAY
For the Children's Sake

Forrest, who was thirteen, would read high school and adult-level history books. Andrew, who was ten, would read intermediate-level books on his own, and he would read easier books aloud to Perry and Thomas, who weren't independent readers yet. They were all studying the same subject but at age-appropriate levels.

Encourage Independent Learning

As soon as my children mastered phonics and became confident readers, I began to encourage independent learning. This was a necessity in our home, but that's not the only reason for doing so. Holding your children's hands academically for too long handicaps them rather than helping them. Karen Andreola explains Charlotte Mason's philosophy: "The more we do for a child the less he will do for himself. If we give him watered-down material, many explanations, much questioning, if we over-moralize, depend on the workbook to work the mind, what thinking is left for the child to do?"[7]

Once again, you have to find the proper balance between independence and the appropriate amount of assistance and instruction. My boys now do most of their studies on their own, and then we use our time together to answer questions and narrate or discuss

> Education must be largely self-initiated, a tapestry woven out of broad experience, constant introspection, ability to concentrate on one's purpose in spite of distractions, a combination of curiosity, patience, and intense watchfulness, and it requires substantial trial and error risk-taking, along with a considerable ability to take feedback from the environment—to learn from mistakes.
> JOHN TAYLOR GATTO
> *Weapons of Mass Instruction*

what they've learned. Forrest says his experience with studying independently prepared him well for college. He has maintained a B average with a full course load and two part-time jobs.

Learning to take responsibility for their own education teaches children important skills that will be useful in college and adult life, gives them opportunities to pursue their own special interests, and encourages them to become lifelong learners.

> The sole true end of education is simply this: to teach men how to learn for themselves.
> DOROTHY SAYERS

Delegate

Homeschooling doesn't necessarily mean that Mom has to be the children's one and only teacher. Delegating part of their instruction to others—inside or outside the family—can add an extra layer of richness to your children's education. Remember that every teacher will be a role model (good or bad) to your children, so delegate wisely.

Your older children can instruct or assist their younger siblings. I always introduce new concepts in math and phonics, but an older child may help a younger child review phonics flashcards, listen to him practice reading aloud, or help him do his map work for geography. Even before he was an independent reader himself, Perry was helping Thomas to learn his letters and numbers and teaching him how to draw simple figures.

This not only gives value to the younger children and frees up some of your time, but it's also good for the older child. Explaining something to someone else is one of the best ways to solidify your own understanding of it. Another sneaky benefit is that reading to younger siblings exposes the older ones to books they might otherwise consider too childish to be worthy of their time. Reading a children's book is a wonderful way to get a simple, well-organized overview or review of a topic.

You can also delegate to carefully chosen instructors outside the family. For example, music is a subject most people find comfortable delegating. Andrew takes piano lessons from an excellent musician in our church. I only wish he had started sooner—I put it off far too long because I kept telling myself I would teach him. I had four years of piano lessons myself and could have gotten him started, but it just never happened.

Consider using instructors in academic subjects as well. Forrest benefitted from both group and private tutoring in math during his high school years. In addition to instructing him, Miss Ann gave him confidence that he really could do math—something I had never been able to accomplish.

If private instructors and tutors don't fit your budget or your lifestyle, consider trading subjects with another homeschool mom in an area you find especially challenging. For example, if you're a math whiz but struggle to teach your children how to write well, find a mom who excels in writing but struggles in math. You can teach math to both her children and yours, and she can teach writing to both her children and yours.

Participating in a homeschool co-op is another way of delegating part of your children's instruction. You have to give up a certain amount

> Lessons outside the home can be a good way to expose your children to a wide variety of new skills and experiences. . . . Individual tutoring is the ideal lesson format for learning. . . . If your child has an exceptional or emerging skill or interest, consider trying to find an older mentor or coach in their area of interest.
>
> CLAY AND SALLY CLARKSON
> *Educating the WholeHearted Child*

of flexibility in exchange for shared planning and instruction, as well as group activities, but the trade-off is worth it for many families. In our co-op, each family studies at home Monday through Thursday and meets for group classes on Friday. Doctors teach high school lab sciences, a nature lover teaches elementary science, a lawyer teaches rhetoric, college instructors teach public speaking and math, and an author/editor (that's me!) teaches literature. All of these teachers are parents of children in our group. Co-ops can be especially helpful for older students, who benefit from the opportunity to present speeches and papers to a live audience and participate in group discussion.

Technological Tutors

Modern technology has given us another way to delegate part of a child's education. My boys have used computer-based curriculum for math, typing, and French. Keep in mind that the younger your children are, the less time they should spend on the computer or watching videos. I'm leery about any curriculum that has students sitting in front of the computer or the DVD player for several hours a day. Use technology with discretion and balance, and don't let it become a substitute for printed books and human interaction.

Audios are my favorite technological tutors. These can be wonderful for learning and reviewing math facts, grammar rules, states and capitals, science terminology, history dates, and so on. Recorded books are a wonderful tool to help you supplement live family read-aloud time. A child who is having difficulty reading can benefit from listening to an audio while following along with the printed book. You can listen to audios individually or as a family while riding in the car, walking around the neighborhood, and doing chores.

My oldest boys used to listen to Diana Waring's history audios, and my younger ones listened to Jim Weiss's storytelling audios at night while drifting off to sleep. For years, Forrest would spout random history facts, and I'd ask, "Where did you learn that?" The answer was either *The Kingfisher Illustrated History of the World* (his preferred bedtime reading) or Diana Waring's *What in the World's Going on Here?* audio series. Consider adding audio to your educational arsenal.

Systematize for Success

In chapter 4 we talked about the difference between a schedule and a routine. Some families work well with a schedule, in which certain things happen at a certain time. Other families work well with a routine in which things don't happen necessarily at a certain time, but they usually happen in a predictable sequence.

Whether you prefer schedules or routines, you need to establish systems for your homeschool. Assign a designated place for the current year's books, notebooks, lesson plans, supplies, and so on. Some families use plastic boxes, drawers, or stackable bins, which works well for younger children. In other families, each child has his own desk and keeps all his books and supplies there. In our home, we keep craft supplies in plastic boxes and use a combination of shelves, notebooks, and stackable trays for everything else. A cubbyhole-style bookcase has designated sections—one for each child, two for shared books and reference books, and two for me. All textbooks, other books, and notebooks belong in the cubbyholes when not in use. This prevents the dreaded "I Can't Find My Math Book" Syndrome.

Each of my boys has a master notebook for the school year with dividers for each subject. Some subjects have a separate notebook, depending on the amount of paperwork involved. Both current and completed assignments go in the notebook. (A three-hole punch is our best friend.) We also keep several shelves of notebooks from past years, providing a nice record of their education. There's no need to save every math worksheet, handwriting lesson, and grammar exercise—we just save representative samples to show progress. We do keep our complete history notebooks for reference and an occasional trip down Memory Lane. In addition to my boys' notebooks, I keep my own homeschool notebook with schedules and phone numbers for our co-op and other activities, a master list of books for each child, and dividers for each subject for each child, including assignments from co-op teachers and photocopies of the tables of contents of their textbooks. Everything I need to plan lessons is thus available in one handy place.

On top of the cubbyholes is a set of stackable trays similar to an inbox/outbox system in an office. Each child has an inbox where I put his assignment sheet and any papers needed for that week's lessons, such as maps, worksheets, or math tests. The boys put their completed work in the top tray, which serves as their outbox and my inbox. After I check their work, I discuss it with them if needed, and they store those pages in their notebooks.

The heart of our system is the weekly assignment sheet. I prefer open-ended documents to boxes (what I want to write never fits in those little spaces), so I simply type all assignments for each child in a Word document. When my boys were younger, I divided each subject into daily assignments; now that they are older, they prefer a weekly list so they can make their own choices about dividing the work (except for math, which needs to be done daily). As long as they finish all assignments for the week by the deadline (Thursday before bedtime, since our co-op meets on Friday), the system works. This teaches them to take responsibility for their own work, and it saves me a lot of time on lesson planning (assigning science chapter 3 for the week is a lot easier than pulling out the textbook and breaking it down into four daily segments with page numbers).

If you're used to micromanaging your children's time, this may sound like a risky plan. Again, it depends on their maturity. When you begin the transition from daily to weekly assignments, be sure to provide guidance to help your children make wise choices. You may be surprised at just how much they are capable of—children will usually rise to meet our expectations. A daily check-in time with Mom helps keep them accountable for staying on track. Whether you use daily or weekly assignment sheets, have children check off each item as they complete it. As we saw with chores in chapter 10, if it's not marked off, it's not yet finished.

Just like your Weekly Plan becomes your record when you review how well you accomplished your goals, the weekly homeschool assignment sheet doubles as a record-keeping system. At the end of the week, evaluate your kids' schoolwork, update the list and print a clean copy if needed, and save it in the binder as a permanent record of their work. Another benefit: When a younger child is covering the same ground in later years, you might be able to copy and paste old assignments instead of starting from scratch.

SAMPLE ASSIGNMENT SHEET FOR 6TH GRADE

Bible
Read Hebrews 7–11
Memorize Hebrews 11:6; review Hebrews 11:3;
    recite in class

History
Listen to song and read Veritas Card 12
The Making of a Knight
Castle (second half)
Eyewitness: Castle
Saint George and the Dragon

Literature
Robin Hood, chapters 14–18
Reading journal

Grammar
Lesson 6

Composition
Lesson 6

Latin
Unit II review
Test on Unit II

Science
Finish reading lesson 5
Write one page about your ocean box project
Continue memorizing Psalm 33:6–9

Math
Lessons 36–42
Quiz 6

SAMPLE ASSIGNMENT SHEET FOR 10TH GRADE

History
Project: family coat of arms
History of Christianity, pages 246–259
Common Roots, The King's Vigil, King Alfred's War Song, Verses by Richard Coeur de
   Lion
IN CLASS: Opportunity 8; Lesson 12: "The Code of Chivalry"

Literature
Beowulf, pages 105–213
Write at least 2 journal entries
AFTER you finish reading *Beowulf*:
Read Seamus Heaney's introduction to his translation (pages ix–xxx). It is a beautifully
   written discussion of the poem and will give you an idea of the issues involved in
   translation.
Read J. R. R. Tolkien's ground-breaking article, "*Beowulf*: The Monsters and the Critics"
Be prepared for class discussion

Composition
Write a characterization on what Grendel's mother would say as she buried her son.

Constitutional Law
Read Articles VI and VII
Read Federalist No. 33 and Anti-Federalist No. 75. Think about the arguments they are
   making for and against the idea of making the Constitution the supreme law of
   the land and what it means to make international treaties equal to the Constitution.
   Be prepared to discuss these ideas in class.
IN CLASS: Articles VI and VII: Supremacy Clause, Oaths, and Ratification

Theology
Knowing God, chapter 6

Chemistry
Read pages 87–98
Answer "On Your Own" questions
Study Guide
CLASS: Module 3 review

Geometry
Lessons 8–11

French
Half an hour a day

More Than Academics

Remember that homeschooling is not just about academics; it's also about building character and nurturing relationships.

When Thomas was four, I had not done much formal schoolwork with him yet. One day he asked, "Is today a school day?" I told him yes. He said, "Well, I want to do school." So I asked, "What kind of schoolwork do you want to do?" He replied, "I want to do the kind of school where the whole family sits down together and draws or reads a story. That's the kind of school I like."

You know, that's the kind of school I like too—where the whole family sits down together and draws or reads a story. Be sure to make room in your life, your week, your day for the whole family sitting down and learning together.

Take Action!

☐ Why do you homeschool? Reminding yourself of your motivations can help you stay the course through hard times.

☐ Do you have realistic expectations for homeschooling? Are your educational approach and schedule a good fit for your family's current circumstances? What changes do you need to make?

☐ Consider how the following options might enhance your homeschooling:

• Teach children of different ages together

- Encourage independent learning

- Delegate

- Use technological tutors

☐ Experiment with a new strategy for homeschooling. For example, if you usually keep a strict schedule, go with the flow for a few days. On the other hand, if the very word *schedule* makes you break out in hives, try following a schedule for a few days. If your children do all their work in the same place every day, head out to the yard or a nearby park. If you haven't read aloud as a family in longer than you care to remember, make it a priority this week.

CHAPTER 14

Solo Act

Flourishing as a Single Mom

A father to the fatherless, a defender of widows,
is God in his holy dwelling.
PSALM 68:5 (NIV)

I wouldn't be honest if I didn't confess that some days I really don't know how I'm going to make it. There's just not enough of me to go around. Sometimes I wrestle with exhaustion, discouragement, loneliness, and frustration. I have discovered, though, that the struggle is hardest when I focus on my circumstances and inadequacies rather than on the love and providence of God. Turning my eyes to Him helps me remember to "be strong in the Lord and in the power of His might" (Ephesians 6:10, NKJV).

Single moms, this chapter is especially for you. My heart goes out to you, for I have been walking this road myself for over a decade. Whether you are widowed, divorced, separated, or never married, I pray that you will find help here. Military deployment of a husband can temporarily bring many of the challenges of single motherhood, so military wives may benefit from this chapter as well.

Married moms, please don't skip this chapter! It's important for you to understand the struggles your single-mom friends and acquaintances are facing. You probably already have a general idea of how tough it is, but I hope to help you understand and minister to them better. I've included a special section at the end of this chapter with practical suggestions for blessing single moms.

Homeschooling can be challenging even under the best of circumstances, but being a single mom increases those challenges exponentially. The economic, physical, spiritual, and emotional support of a husband is subtracted from the equation, and the work is multiplied. Single moms often struggle with grief, guilt, shame, exhaustion, fear, poverty, loneliness, and discouragement.

The increasing number of single parents choosing to educate their children at home, however, testifies that it can work. Brian Ray of the National Home Education Research Institute told me his studies show that about two percent of homeschooling families are headed by single parents, but it is his opinion that this figure probably underrepresents the true number.

Rest in God's Faithfulness

None of us, single or married, can homeschool by relying on our own power. But God's grace is sufficient for us, for His strength is made perfect in our weakness (2 Corinthians 12:9).

As my pastor reminded us in a sermon, suffering shifts our hope from something that is uncertain to something that is certain. For a long time I had unconsciously found security in my circumstances. As a single mom, I had to rely on God in a new way. I knew that God had called me to be at home with my children, so I trusted that He would continue providing the means for this to happen. Even with all the systems and routines I've described, things don't always go exactly as planned. But through God's grace, my children are growing, learning, and flourishing right here at home with me. I wouldn't want it any other way.

> The steadfast love of the Lord never ceases; his mercies never come to an end; they are new every morning; great is your faithfulness.
> LAMENTATIONS 3:22–23 (ESV)

If God has called you to homeschool your children, He will provide you the strength, patience, grace, resources, and time to do it. Let your family and your life be a testimony of God's faithfulness.

You're Still a Family

Little girls don't dream of growing up to be single moms. Losing a spouse to death, desertion, or divorce alters the family structure so profoundly that it can be hard to think of yourself as a real family, especially when you're labeled as a "broken family" and you hear about the hazards of fatherless homes. Single moms of girls wonder how their daughters will learn to relate to men, while single mothers of boys wonder where their sons will find godly male role models.

The homeschool culture's focus on building strong marriages and the role of the father can unintentionally compound this sense of insecurity. Please understand: I am not saying this emphasis is wrong; on the contrary, it's a worthy goal to help build strong families and keep them together. However, if you're already feeling vulnerable and fragile because you have been widowed, abused, or abandoned, this focus can often be discouraging and depressing.

If you're the only single mom in a church, co-op, or homeschool support group, it can be easy to feel like you don't fit in. So many women have told me about their struggles in this area. It helps to focus on what you have in common rather than your differences. I often have more in common with a married homeschooling mom who doesn't have a home business than I do with a single career woman or mom with a job and her kids in public school. But I also have things in common with that single career woman and public-school mom, and we can be friends and encourage one another. Friends don't have to be just like you.

I am blessed with a wonderful support network of friends, family, and church, and I usually feel pretty strong. However, in my seventh year as a single mom—after I had long since adjusted to a new "normal"—I cried in the car all the way home from our co-op's back-to-school meeting. Why? Because all the other moms' husbands were carrying their boxes of books to the car for them. I'm perfectly capable of carrying my own books, but the boxes weren't the point. On a dark night after a long, hard day, that one seemingly insignificant image broke me. It symbolized all that I lack. It's not that I was envious. I was just lonely.

> The Lord your God in your midst, The Mighty One, will save; He will rejoice over you with gladness, He will quiet you with His love, He will rejoice over you with singing.
> ZEPHANIAH 3:17 (NKJV)

While it's natural to feel sad or vulnerable from time to time, be careful not to become defensive or oversensitive. If you have been wounded by unkind words or critical people, you may be quick to take offense and assume that others are judging you or don't care about you. However, this kind of prickliness can become a self-fulfilling prophecy by driving people away. Ask yourself honestly if you have a chip on your shoulder, and extend to others the same grace you'd like to receive from them.

If you're newly single, take heart: It does get easier. It takes time to adjust and find a new "normal," but it's essential to establish a new family identity despite all the changes. Don't settle for feeling second-class.

Foster a Strong Sense of Family Identity and Unity

Your children will take their cues from you. Hard as it is, you have to lead the way in establishing a new family identity. Be discreet in how you talk around them; don't complain about how others treat or perceive you. You might end up making your children hypersensitive in situations where they were previously comfortable. If you are divorced, avoid criticizing your ex-husband within their earshot. After all, he's still their dad. If you need to talk through your struggles, pour out your heart to a trustworthy friend and to God.

Don't neglect to make time for having fun as a family. If you work at home, it is especially difficult to identify when your work day is over. I know just how hard it can be to pull away when deadlines are looming and the electric bill is due, but as we saw in chapter 9, taking a break is good for you as well as your children, and it can actually make your work time more efficient. Family fun doesn't have to be expensive. Visit a local park, have a picnic, watch a DVD together, make s'mores, or read a good book together.

Holidays can be tough, especially during the initial transition. Keep up old family traditions and establish new ones as well. For example, my boys and I celebrate Christmas just as we always have, with the addition of visiting their dad and grandparents on Christmas afternoon. If you're separated from your children on holidays, don't give in to the temptation to wallow in loneliness. Enjoy the hospitality of friends or serve others through hospitality or ministry. If your children are gone for Thanksgiving, for example, you might invite other single moms who are childless for the holiday to your home for a potluck feast, or you might help serve Thanksgiving dinner at the local homeless shelter. There's nothing like helping someone going through a harder time than you are to make you grateful for what you have.

Don't Be a Lone Ranger

A support network is helpful for any homeschooler, but it's particularly crucial for single parents, who lack the help and sounding board of a spouse. We need someone to talk through challenges with us and sometimes give us a shoulder to cry on.

Get involved in a local church and ask folks there to pray for you. Seek out a homeschool support group in your area. Nurture godly friendships. I frequently consult a few close friends about choices in training and educating my children and seek advice on business matters from fellow Christian entrepreneurs who share my family-based priorities.

> Trust the past to God's mercy, the present to God's love and the future to God's providence.
> AUGUSTINE

Don't be afraid or too proud to ask for the help you need. It's wonderful when someone helps without being asked, but people may not know what you need, or they may feel uncomfortable about offering. Many people are happy to help when asked, and they will be blessed themselves by ministering to you. My church does a wonderful job of helping single parents, and many others do so as well.

Sadly, some churches seem unwilling to help. I've heard some distressing stories from single moms who have been shunned, criticized, and wounded by their churches. Sometimes it's best to simply find a new church home. One dear friend found support and encouragement from her new church family after years of going it alone. When people fail you, remember that God is always faithful.

Make Homeschooling Work

Pressing on with homeschooling despite the trauma of death or divorce provides continuity and stability for children in a situation that has rocked their world. It allows them to hold on to something familiar instead of being sent to spend their days in a strange new environment, creating even more upheaval in their lives. The flexibility of homeschooling allows them time to heal and may simplify visitation with the noncustodial parent.

Someone may have told you, "Homeschooling is nice, but there's no way you can do it on your own. You need to put the kids in school and get a real job." Most people have good intentions, but it's important to consider the source. Is this person generally opposed to homeschooling anyway? Does she understand homeschooling in all its variety and flexibility? Rather than being discouraged by the naysayers, seek out wise counsel from people who love you and are willing to help you explore your options and support you whatever your decision.

No one needs to find peace in the space between the ideal and reality more than a single mom. Be realistic in your expectations for homeschooling, particularly about how much time you can devote to direct instruction of your children. You will probably have to make some changes, but that's OK. It may not be possible for your homeschool to match your highest goals, but you can still make it work. Chapter 13 includes lots of ideas for teaching your children to be independent learners.

Balance Work and Family

The necessity of providing for our families financially, as well as training and educating our children, often presents the biggest challenge to single moms. Working from home is a good option if you can make it happen.

As we've already seen, it's important to balance accessibility with boundaries. You need to teach your children to be responsible and, depending on their ages, independent. Some kinds of work can be done in the midst of busy, noisy family life, but others require quiet time alone. You can work before your children wake up, during their naptime, and after they go to bed, but don't overdo it—you need adequate sleep to handle all your responsibilities and challenges. If your children visit their father or grandparents, take advantage of that solo time by focusing on your work to free up more of your time when the kids are at home.

Especially if your children are young, you may need to enlist childcare while you work. Here are a few options: Swap childcare with another single mom. Rely on volunteers such as grandparents, friends, or people from church. Depending on your income, it may be a wise financial decision to hire a babysitter or mother's helper to care for your children while you work. One single mom I know was able to take an older child to her office, where he studied quietly while she worked.

If your work cannot be done at home, perhaps you can rearrange your schedule to maximize your time at home. A friend who lost his wife to cancer shifted his work schedule as a piano tuner to two ten- to twelve-hour days a week so that he could be home with his two young sons most days. He hired homeschool graduates to care for his boys on his work days, and his mother and sisters helped out as well. Because he was working more efficiently with this concentrated schedule, he was still earning about 75 percent of his previous full-time income.

If having a home business appeals to you, you'll find much more helpful information in chapter 15.

My husband had just left us, and I was still in panic/crisis mode. I was put on partial bed rest due to pregnancy complications with baby #4. However, by using time-management and goal-setting techniques, I was still able to homeschool my children, prepare meals, maintain the house and handle minor repairs, start writing again, care for my handicapped mother, and tend to my own needs. And I will soon have my first website up. The kids have noticed a huge change in me as well. They are no longer interrupting when I'm on the phone, they have become more self-sufficient (only one pink sock since they took over the laundry!) and they are learning more about family unity. Everyone helps rather than Mom doing it all, and their confidence has grown so much.
ROBIN, single mom from Texas

Take Care of Yourself

Most single parents I've talked with neglect taking care of themselves. It's easy to do when your responsibilities seem like more than one person can handle, but you simply can't nurture, provide for, and educate your children well if you're always on the verge of burnout.

Taking care of yourself isn't selfish, and it isn't optional. To be able to handle all your responsibilities, you absolutely must make time for personal rest, renewal, relaxation, and even recreation. Make sure you're getting enough sleep, exercising, eating right, and drinking plenty of water.

If your children visit their father or grandparents, that's a good opportunity make some time for yourself. When I was first divorced and my boys would leave home to visit their dad, I would find myself moping and wandering aimlessly around the house. Then I realized that what I had was, in a strange way, a gift of some built-in silence and solitude with no urgent demands on my attention. As I mentioned earlier, these visits can be a good time to work in your business, but be sure to allow yourself a bit of a break too—perhaps lunch with a friend, a movie, or a couple of hours with a good book. If you're a widow, you won't have this built-in break, but perhaps your children can spend time with grandparents, friends, or church members so you can have some quiet time alone now and then.

So many of the single parents I talk with seem to need permission to take care of themselves. If that describes you, I want to officially give you permission right now! It's not only OK; it's essential.

Remember that although the days are long and difficult, the years of bringing up children on your own are only a season. As your children grow older, they will become more responsible and independent, which will lighten your burden. Above all, lean on God's mercy, strength, and faithfulness.

How You Can Help a Single-Parent Family

"Religion that God our Father accepts as pure and faultless is this: to look after orphans and widows in their distress and to keep oneself from being polluted by the world" (James 1:27, NIV). The Bible contains many commands and examples relating to caring for the needy, but James 1:27 would be enough even if it stood alone. My former pastor, Tim Fortner, explained our church's commitment to single-parent families this way:

> We take seriously the covenantal implications of caring for all the members of the church in a family context. The whole congregation takes vows to help with the children—not only to be an example, but also to meet particular needs of modeling, encouragement, and financial support. The need is expanded when the father is not there. Galatians 6:10 tells us, "So then, while we have opportunity, let us do good to all people, and especially to those who are of the household of the faith."

Ministry to widows may be broadened to include those who are single through divorce or desertion. The church's obligation to orphans extends to children in homes without both parents present, for whatever reason, including military deployment.

Sadly, in our fallen world, single-parent families abound. They live in the house around the corner, stand next to you in line at the grocery store, and occupy the adjacent pew at church. How can you follow the biblical injunction to "look after" these parents and their children? Be sensitive to their situation, and remember to offer EMT (encouragement, material help, and time).

WALK A MILE IN HER MOCCASINS

I asked single moms, "What is hardest for you about being a single mom and homeschooling?" Here are some of the challenges they shared, in their own words:

- "The main thing for me is the unreliable financial support and the emotional strain on me personally of not having a spouse. Dealing with the emotional fallout with the kids is a challenge too."

- "Having to work a full- and part-time job on top of homeschooling. Having to homeschool differently from when I was married and could just be a stay-at-home mom and concentrate on homeschooling."

- "Pushing through the exhaustion to teach and spend time with my little blessing so that he gets what he needs on a daily basis."

- "Encouragement for both me and my child. She loves being asked what she's been doing and learning. I had to tell my parents that I needed them to inquire about what I was doing and to see if there was anything I needed or needed to talk out. It's really helped me stay confident in what I'm doing just knowing there's some support."

- "Most of the families at our church homeschool, but they never include us when they go to the park or get together for crafts. Always after the fact they say, 'Oh! You should have come!' Um, I didn't know anything about it. People just aren't sure how to get their head around my homeschooling as a single mom."

- "Having the pressure of earning an income and schooling children at the same time. Thank God for my friends who help out."

Be Sensitive to Their Concerns and Needs

Far too many single moms have been wounded by their churches, friends, and homeschool support groups. Some are now afraid to ask for help because they have been accused of being lazy or feeling entitled, but most are doing the best they can. Some have been hurt by people who assume that single moms are promiscuous and divorcées are to blame for the failure of their own marriages. Whatever a single parent's circumstances, be careful not to jump to conclusions. They are hurting and they need your help. Some have become defensive and prickly. Love them anyway, and help them anyway.

Be cautious about saying that you understand what it's like to be a single mom because your husband is hardly ever at home because he works long hours or travels for business. You mean to show sympathy, but this statement can easily backfire. A hurting single mom may focus on the fact that your faithful husband is providing for his family and does come home sometimes. Remember that unless you've been divorced or widowed yourself, you probably don't have any real idea what single moms are going through 24/7/365.

As I mentioned earlier, the homeschool culture's emphasis on marriage and fathers, while important, can be painful for women whose husbands have died or deserted them. This is not to say that authors and speakers should walk on eggshells; not every statement about God's design for the family needs a footnote for single parents. It's a real challenge to focus on the best while still ministering to those who do not experience it, for whatever reason. I simply encourage you to be sensitive about how easily single parents can be wounded, to be cautious about inadvertently excluding them when writing or speaking about the family, and to look for ways to minister to them directly. I've recently noticed a welcome trend toward acknowledging and encouraging single parents. For example, Sarah Mae and Sally Clarkson include a special note to single moms in *Desperate: Hope for the Mom Who Needs to Breathe*. Israel Wayne's *Full-Time Parenting: A Guide to Family-Based Discipleship* includes a chapter of "Comfort and Advice for Single Parents" written by his mother, Skeet Savage. Both of these books are excellent.

I feel that my ex divorcing me exiled me into a separate place from other Christians. I think this might be partly because I spend almost no time with other single moms (they're all working) and partly because I have experienced judgment and suspicion from Christians who know only one thing about me: I'm divorced. It's very disturbing to feel alienated from the body of Christ.
SINGLE HOMESCHOOLING MOM

Offer Encouragement, Prayer, and Counsel

Parenting is always a demanding job, and it's doubly challenging for those who tackle it alone. Praying faithfully for single-parent families is one of the most important ways you can minister to them. Letting these families know you are holding them up in prayer multiplies the blessing. Single parents often feel overwhelmed and discouraged, so make sure to praise the positive things in their lives and encourage them not to grow weary in doing good. Their children need encouragement too. One man in our church sent my boys a note praising the way they honor God by their behavior in church and their helpfulness to me. Such support inspired them to continue to grow spiritually.

Without a spouse to help make decisions regarding childrearing, finances, and other challenges, single parents need wise, godly counsel. A newly single mother whose husband previously handled all the family finances may need instruction in planning a budget and being a good steward of her resources, or she may need assistance in finding ways to earn an income, preferably from home.

Offer Material Help

Many single parents need financial help, especially during the immediate transition after a death or divorce. Life insurance or child support and alimony—if they exist at all—often fall far short of meeting a family's basic needs. Single-parent families, especially those headed by women, often rank among the country's poorest.

Our church's deacons fund has provided monetary aid to my family several times, especially in the early years when I was building my business and my income fluctuated significantly. In addition, individual church members sent us cash and gift cards, sometimes routing these blessings through the church office to remain anonymous. God's providential care has clearly orchestrated the timing of such help. During seasons of comparative bounty, financial gifts rarely arrived. However, when we did need help, assistance miraculously appeared, even when I told no one about our situation.

Once a $100 gift card to a department store arrived in the mail with instructions to use it for myself, not my children. This happened shortly before an entrepreneurs' conference where I was scheduled to speak. The gift was more than enough for the new suit I needed, and it served as a precious reminder of God's faithfulness in clothing not only the lilies of the field, but also His children.

You can also help by sharing material things, both new and used. Several families regularly handed down their children's clothing to my boys, and when my youngest child outgrew the clothes, we passed them along to others. One sweet lady blessed me with three beautiful new outfits.

One year a family in our church gave us a brand-new train table for the boys to use with their wooden train set, saving me the time and expense of Christmas shopping as well. Another friend thoughtfully asked me for a list of my children's favorite Christmas candy so she could fill their stockings every year. Our pastor taught me how to build a fire in our woodstove, and several men in the church have faithfully kept us supplied with firewood for eleven years.

Offer Your Time

The gift of time can be a tremendous blessing. After a year of commuting to church twice weekly from an hour away, I decided to move closer to the church. Several ladies helped me pack my kitchen, and others helped me clean the new house before we moved in. Church members helped load, move, and unload our belongings. Throughout moving day, at least ten men helped, while two ladies cared for my children in their homes. When my parents gave us a wooden swing set for Christmas, several men volunteered their time in the evenings to assemble it. At one point a doctor, a banker, an accountant, and an engineer were all working together in our back yard, and they took extra time to let my boys help.

For several months, one dear lady from the church came to our house for two to three hours once a week so that I could go to the grocery store and run other errands without four boys in tow. When she had to take a break due to back trouble, another woman—whom I barely knew at the time—offered to take her place. These women became my friends and blessed me immeasurably, but they also ministered to my children by reading to them, playing games with them, bringing them treats, and showing them God's love. We were likewise blessed when a summer youth worker who wanted to teach the young people in our church to serve others encouraged the older teens to provide us with free babysitting.

Another opportunity for ministry is including single-parent families in special events or outings and holiday celebrations, which can be particularly difficult during the transition to singleness. Keep in mind, too, that some single parents may be alone for the holidays when their children are visiting the other parent. That can be a particularly lonely time when joining another family's celebration would be welcome.

My boys and I have fond memories of an Independence Day cookout with several other families. The children enjoyed shelter-building and corn-shucking contests, and the men and boys competed in tree-chopping and shooting matches. The men taught my boys how to shoot and my oldest how to swing an axe. Having fun with these other families was so refreshing, and this was a great opportunity for my sons to learn some manly skills.

One of the greatest ways you can serve single-parent families is to mentor their children. Daughters of single fathers will benefit from training in womanly arts and biblical femininity, while sons of single mothers need godly men to show them the true meaning of biblical manhood. Although ongoing mentoring relationships prove especially helpful, short-term projects can also be a blessing. An engineer from our church took my mathematically inclined son (age nine at the time) to help him survey the church parking lot. He taught Andrew about the surveying instruments and reported enthusiastically about Andrew's skill as a rod man. Forrest has enjoyed sailing with our pastor, and he received far more than seamanship skills from the time they spent together.

WHAT SINGLE MOMS NEED

I've been extraordinarily blessed with support and assistance from family, friends, and church. Sadly, many single moms have not been so blessed. When I asked online groups of single homeschooling moms how people have helped them—and how they wish people would help—they shared the ideas below. I've sorted their answers into the EMT categories but kept their words so you can hear their voices and get a glimpse into their hearts.

ENCOURAGEMENT

- Ask us how we are (when you really have time to listen).

- Encourage us in front of our kids. Tell us we're doing a good job and encourage our children to work hard, respect Mom, and trust her decisions.

- Call with a word of encouragement or prayer.

- Don't disappear—keep in touch every so often.

- A big, big bonus would be for someone to ask me to sit with them during church. It doesn't bother me when I have the kids, but it's so awkward to sit all alone when they are not with me!

- I often feel I am the only one speaking biblical truth to my kids (besides Sunday School classes), so I love it when others share their faith or encourage my kids in their faith. I want them to see Jesus in others too.

- Tell me I'm doing a great job. Compliment the good qualities you see in my kids. As a single mom, I question every little decision I make and how it will impact my kids. Compliments can help build my confidence.

MATERIAL HELP

- Lend or donate curriculum and other homeschool resources.

- Call to say, "Hey, I'm at the grocery store. Is there anything I can pick up for you?"

- Give a gift card for a fun family outing—a movie at the theater, bowling, a day at the beach, etc. These outings are often more than we can afford, but they would give us a break from the daily stress and add such joy to our lives.

- Bring over a pizza or a hot meal—just because!

- Sometimes other homeschooling families buy season passes or memberships to places like zoos, YMCAs, museums, etc. Giving us unused passes (if they are transferrable) or bringing us along as guests might be an option.

- Pass along clothes for the kids.

- Every year for Christmas, a precious couple used to give me a gift card to our local shopping center. Their generosity helped us out so much.

TIME

- Invite and include our kids in activities when possible. Those extra events—play dates, gym days, field trips, etc.—suffer the most for us, as I am working when such activities happen.

- Connect us with people who could mentor/apprentice our children.

- Have us over for play dates (many are isolated) and dinner (money is tight!).

- If you're doing an experiment or project, ask us to join you.

- Be willing to support our children's efforts to exercise skill by attending an informal presentation night, talent show, etc.

- Provide transportation for children's activities to help me save both time and gas money.

- This one might be the most important. Include my children in your normal activities. Sometimes they feel like social outcasts because they are stuck with the single mom. If your husband is taking your children fishing, invite mine along. Above all else, my children want to feel *normal*. So don't invite us as a charity thing; invite us as *friends*.

- Offer to have your husband check our oil, tune up the lawn mower, or load a moving van.

- Take us to a funny movie. (Laughter is a great stress reliever.)

- Provide a male role model for my boys. I have one friend whose husband always makes a big fuss over my boys . . . making them feel special. My boys are young (1 and 3), but as they get older, I'd love for some godly men to say, "Can I take Alexander with me to help fix such and such?" giving them time with a godly man while also learning productive skills!

- Offer to babysit and be clear that no reciprocating is necessary.

- Invite us over for a family game night (not just moms/kids—having positive male influences for our kids is so necessary).

- A friend of mine (who has similar-aged, homeschooled children) occasionally asks if we can join them for lunch, then stay for science experiments that they have planned or another school activity. This kills two birds with one stone for me—social activity combined with academics for the kids—that I didn't have to plan!

Take the Initiative

If you want to help a single mom, don't wait for her to ask. She may be embarrassed to ask for help. Volunteer your assistance or ask what she needs. Often there's a flurry of help soon after a death or divorce, but it typically fades away after a few months, so keep offering.

Be sensitive to the prompting of the Holy Spirit. I have been amazed at the multitude of creative ways in which people have ministered to my family, and especially at God's providence in meeting our needs at just the right time. Don't be concerned if you can't help financially—there are many other ways you can bless single parents and their children. One mom summed it up well, saying, "Single moms appreciate every little encouragement or gift if it's given with love."

Take Action!

FOR SINGLE MOMS:

☐ Are you resting in God's faithfulness? How can you remind yourself each day to lean on Him?

☐ Are you sometimes defensive or oversensitive? Make a commitment to extend to others the same grace and understanding you'd like to receive from them.

☐ How are you fostering a strong sense of family identity and unity? Plan a regular time to have fun as a family.

☐ Are you trying to go it alone, or do you have a support network? Don't hesitate to ask for the help you need.

☐ What are some practical ways that you can make homeschooling work as a single mom?

❐ What is one thing you can do to help balance your work and family responsibilities?

❐ Are you taking care of yourself? What's one thing you can do this week to put on your own oxygen mask?

FOR MARRIED MOMS:

❐ Are you sensitive to the concerns and needs of single moms? How can you be more loving?

❐ Choose at least one single mom to bless in a special way. Consider how you can minister to her in these ways:

- Encouragement, prayer, and counsel

- Material help

- Time

CHAPTER 15

Home Business

*She makes linen garments and sells them, and supplies
belts to the tradesmen.*
PROVERBS 31:24

Dave Mitchell was working ten to twelve hours a day as an electrical controls designer in Tennessee. With a forty-five-minute commute each way, he didn't have nearly enough time with his six sons. He and his wife, Kay, prayed about starting a home business. When he was laid off from his job, they started selling health products. He took another controls designing job for a while, but his heart was still at home. Joshua, their oldest son, was learning computer programming, and he and his father began attending business conferences together. Dave bought some audio recording supplies and learned how to record teleseminars and live events.

In 2003, Dave came home full time, and the whole family got involved in their new business, Recorded Moments. As the boys grew older, they learned to record speakers at conferences and teleseminars, answer the phone for business calls, duplicate and ship recordings, and network with prospective clients at events. Running a business became part of their homeschool adventure. They read and listened to audiobooks while traveling around the country to record business conferences, and they also learned from the men and women they were recording. The business grew to include Kay's sister, and they eventually hired a bookkeeper/virtual assistant to help with customer support.

In January 2007, Dave became ill and was diagnosed with liver cancer. He died only two and a half months later. "Time and time again, I can see how the Lord took care of us," Kay says. "God gave Dave that time with the boys to teach them so much they wouldn't have learned if he had kept his old job. Having a family business was such a blessing because when he died, we could continue, and I didn't have to worry about going out and getting a job or worry about whether we could continue homeschooling. I could rest in the fact that God had provided this business for us." What a powerful story of God's faithfulness!

As the Mitchells learned and more and more families are discovering, home business blends well with homeschooling. The two share many of the same benefits, including a life centered on home and family, freedom to focus on your own interests, and flexibility to arrange work and activities to suit your unique lifestyle. Whether you already have a home business or are thinking about starting one, this chapter will help you consider what might work for you and your family. This is a very broad overview, so be sure to check out the additional resources listed in appendix A.

Why Have a Home Business?

Running a home-based business requires skill, diligence, commitment, and endurance. It's not easy, but it comes with many benefits.

FINANCES

In these tough economic times, it's becoming harder and harder for families to survive on one income, no matter how committed and frugal they are. However, that doesn't mean you have to quit homeschooling and take a job outside the home. A home business may be a way for Mom to help provide for the family while remaining at home, a way to bring Dad home, or even a way for the children to learn entrepreneurship as the whole family works together.

FREEDOM

Having your own business allows you the freedom to follow your dreams, pursue your passions, and make a living from what you love doing. As your own boss, you call the shots. You choose what to do and when and where to work. However, this is not for the faint of heart. Entrepreneurship is risky. But in today's world, there is no such thing as job security even when you have a steady job with a long-time employer.

FLEXIBILITY

When you're employed by someone else, you lose control of your time. Maybe you have an 8-to-5 office job, or you switch between day and night shifts, or your schedule fluctuates every week so that you can't plan ahead. As an entrepreneur, you set your own schedule. You have to take your customers' and clients' needs into consideration, but you can design your business to accommodate the life you want. Many businesses are flexible in location as well as time, allowing you to relocate or travel as you wish and take your business with you.

FUTURE

Working in the family business enhances your children's home education and teaches them important, practical, real-world skills. Some home businesses turn into multigenerational enterprises that your children—and maybe even your grandchildren—can carry on after you. They can also be a way for a mom to support her family while remaining at home and continuing to homeschool, even if something happens to her husband.

Options for Home Business

In an increasingly digital world, the possibilities for earning a living from home are almost endless. Home business may include work *at* home (you don't have to leave your house to do the work, such as working for a call center) or work *from* home (home is your base of operations, but you sometimes leave to do projects elsewhere, such as mystery shopping). You can work for a company as an employee or an independent contractor, or you can create your own business.

Working at home for someone else's business can include telecommuting, work-at-home jobs such as tech support or customer service, or working with a multilevel marketing company such as Amway or Pampered Chef. You don't have to start a business from scratch, but you'll have less flexibility working for someone else. This is an acceptable trade-off for many people.

Running your own business puts all the burden and expense on you but provides more flexibility and often greater potential for profit. There are two general categories of things you can sell: products or services. Products can be things you create or things someone else created. You can sell products on eBay, on your website, or through affiliate links on your blog. Physical products include such things as handcrafted furniture, hand-knit sweaters, baked goods, and produce from your garden. Information products such as books, curriculum, and home study courses can be physical and/or digital. Services include writing, editing, transcribing, website design, virtual assistance, tech support, cleaning, accounting, yard work, sewing, music, lessons, tutoring, home repair, pet-sitting, running errands, and much more.

Which Business Is Right for You?

How do you figure out what kind of home business is right for you? Consider your Big Dream, and look back at the section on focus in chapter 3. What are you passionate about? What are your most profitable skills? What is unique about what you have to offer? Who wants to buy what you want to sell?

This is yet another area requiring balance: You have to consider both your passion and market demand. If you sell what the market demands but you hate every minute of it, you'll be miserable. If you try to sell what you love but nobody wants to buy it, you'll soon be broke. For example, a friend of mine spent a lot of time and money a few years ago learning how to create Google AdSense sites. He made a lot of money, but he was bored and absolutely hated it. It might be just the right thing for someone else, but he realized his heart wasn't in it, and that's not the way he wanted to build his business. He quit working with AdSense and turned his focus to something he loved: using his accounting and business background to help entrepreneurs successfully manage the administrative side of running a profitable business.

> When love and skill work together, expect a masterpiece.
> JOHN RUSKIN
> Victorian artist and critic

On the other hand, if your passion is underwater basket weaving and you're the world's leading expert on underwater basket weaving, and you create the finest e-book or the finest home study course ever created in all of human history on underwater basket weaving, well . . . let's face it, nobody's going to buy it.

You have to make sure you balance your passion with what the market is looking for. The basic steps for creating a successful business in a nutshell—the secrets you've been waiting for—are as follows:

1. Find a problem.

2. Solve it.

3. Sell the solution.

One way to find a problem to solve is market research. You can do keyword research online, look at magazines and books, see what's in the news, or conduct online surveys. Both my "How Do You Do It All?" course and this book were significantly shaped by responses to surveys.

But once you know there's a demand, how do you choose which problem you should solve? In addition to considering your interests, passions, experience, and skills, one great way to figure out what your focus should be is to think about what people ask you about most often. Do they ask you how to teach Spanish to children, how to be a great hostess, how to save money, how to cook healthy meals, how to create a homeschool transcript, or how to travel on a budget? This strategy worked really well for me. The number one question people have asked me for years is "How do you do it all?" My course was the answer to that question. Another common question people ask me is "How can I start my own editing business?" So I created a course called "Get Started as a Freelance Editor: Skills, Strategies, and Resources" (which you can find at www.EditingBusiness.com). Another question I'm often asked is "How do I write a book?" Yes, I'm in the process of creating a book or course about that as well.

Entrepreneurs are often creative and multitalented—this is both a blessing and a challenge. If you have interests, talents, and marketable solutions in several different areas, you'll need to pick one to focus on first. You can't do a good job of trying to launch three different businesses at one time. You may launch them one after another, but you're going to get the most mileage for your time, effort, and attention by focusing on just one thing at first.

One way to narrow your focus is to consider which option will produce income the soonest. Consider your start-up costs, ongoing expenses, and potential profit. This isn't always the best long-term strategy for building a business, but as you're getting started, it can be useful. The cash flow from that initial venture can also help fund the development of your other business ideas down the road.

It's also important to consider your unique selling proposition (USP). How are you different from other people who are selling the same thing or something similar? What makes your product or service special? Why should a prospective client or customer choose you over your competition? For example, my primary business is editing books and coaching authors. Plenty of people can correct typos, spelling, grammar, and punctuation, and lots of high school English teachers are willing to proof manuscripts. One thing that sets me apart is my familiarity with the larger issues of publishing and marketing, so working with me is appealing to entrepreneurs and speakers who want to write a book to grow their businesses. Many of them lack confidence about their writing ability, so I often say "I'll help you author a book, whether or not you can write." (Visit www.WriteAGreatBook.com for more information.)

Getting Started

The most common question people ask me about having their own business is "How do I get started?" One mom said, "I struggle with feeling like I have to have everything together to get the business off the ground." Many others feel the same way. But if you truly have to have *everything* together to get your business off the ground, you'll probably never get started.

Of course it's important to think and research and plan—starting a business is not something to take lightly or jump into blindly. But don't wait for all the conditions to be perfect. What can you do now with what you have now where you are now?

Two of the major obstacles to getting started are fitting in a business along with all your existing responsibilities and surviving financially while you build up your new business. We've already talked about dozens of strategies for managing your responsibilities. For example, don't forget that to add something new, you'll need to eliminate, delegate, or outsource something you're currently doing. Life may actually get harder before it gets easier when you're trying to do a new thing, so don't let that take you by surprise. The get-rich-quick gurus fail to mention this. I've heard people say, "Your computer is an ATM. Just grab the cash out of it." Computers and the Internet certainly expand the range of options for home business. But like any ATM, you can only withdraw what you deposit.

> I never won anything without hard labor and the exercise of my best judgment and careful planning and working long in advance.
> THEODORE ROOSEVELT
> *An Autobiography*

If you're shifting from employment to self-employment or from one business to another, the transition can be tough. You'll usually have to work more before you can work less. For example, at first my business was strictly service-based. I edited books. At entrepreneur conferences I learned about the profit potential of creating my own products, but it takes a while for the income to start coming in from these products. Oddly enough, the electric company and grocery store don't accept e-books in lieu of payment, so I had to continue editing to pay the bills while I began teaching classes and creating courses and books to generate long-term income streams.

The Learning Curve

The learning curve is another challenge. You already have some knowledge about your field, but maybe you need to learn new skills, or maybe you need to learn more about the details of running a business. "Educate" is one of the strategies in our FREEDOM toolbox, but you won't get paid directly for the time you spend learning. You have to learn *and* do simultaneously. Take action by implementing what you learn.

You don't have to learn how to do *everything* yourself, though. Consider delegating or outsourcing some tasks in lieu of learning a specific skill yourself so that you can focus on more important and profitable activities. One of my coaching clients has one family member who knows how to design websites and do keyword research and two others who know how to do photography and create videos. She thought she needed to learn these skills herself, but I advised her to use her family members' expertise and focus on what only she can do.

There *is* such a thing as having too much information. I'm an information junkie, so that's a really hard confession for me to make. Learning is important, but it can become an excuse for procrastination. You don't have to learn every single aspect of a business to get started. Begin with what you know, and learn (or outsource) new skills when you need them.

And keep learning as long as you live. Invest in your business by investing in yourself through books, home study courses, teleseminars, private coaching, and conferences. Then take action on what you're learning as you go.

What Can You Outsource?

If you can't learn and do everything yourself, the first step is simply acknowledging your need to outsource something in your business. Entrepreneurs are naturally independent and self-sufficient, so admitting this can be harder than you might think.

An online entrepreneurs group was discussing the day-to-day details of running a business, particularly duplicating CDs. One person commented that doing it yourself can cost almost as much as hiring it out—that basically you pay for the privilege of sitting there doing it yourself. Whether it's making CDs or copying and binding books or filling orders, it's important to consider the value—the actual cash value—of your time. The most successful people I know follow this simple principle:

Focus on what you do best and what brings the most value for your time, and outsource everything else.

For example, if you're a software developer, you might spend your time brainstorming and designing new programs and hire someone else to handle customer service. If you're a self-published author, you should focus your efforts on writing and promoting new books and let someone else process and ship orders.

I once heard Armand Morin, a brilliant businessman, say that he loves designing graphics for his websites, but he doesn't do it himself because his time is much better spent coming up with ideas for new products. When I mentioned this online, someone responded with criticism: "If he loves it, he shouldn't have to pay somebody else to do it." But few people can do everything they love; we all have to choose the best use of our time. Armand also loves creating products, so he wasn't sacrificing a passion to do something less fulfilling. It was a reasonable decision for him to make.

Whether or not your business budget currently allows for outsourcing, ask yourself these questions:

1. What is it that only I can do?

2. What do I do best?

3. What's the most profitable use of my time?

4. What can I hire someone else to do to free my time to focus on numbers 1–3?

An author of homeschool curriculum told me, "If I had known what I know now when we started our business, I would have handled some of the materials differently so that they weren't so dependent on our babysitting e-mails. I'd also make the process easier for a fulfillment house to handle. Right now I wouldn't trust one due to the various levels of problems that can come from manufacturers such as missing CDs and cases, occasional bad printing of a page, etc."

Quality control is a legitimate concern anytime you outsource something. But I encouraged her to think about how else she could handle this. Is she the only person on the planet who can check for missing CDs or improper printing of a page? Could she create guidelines for someone else to follow? It can be hard to find good help; don't always look for the lowest bid. Trustworthy contractors and assistants can be worth their weight in gold.

For me, working from home was no dream. It had become more like a nightmare! Long hours, competing demands, unrealistic expectations (primarily my own), mom guilt, and physical exhaustion had pushed me to the edge of burnout. But these organizational principles brought clarity to my situation. I've been empowered to make foundational changes, both in the way I think and in the way I work. For instance, instead of stressing that I don't have the time to do something, I'll ask myself "How can I find the time to do this?" When I look at the goals and priorities I have set and the schedule I've created, I may decide that I don't need or want to do it at all!

ELEANOR JOYCE, Pennsylvania

Generating Income

Business is about making money, or generating income. If you're not making money, it's a hobby and not a business (at least according to the IRS).

Don't confuse business with ministry. Many Christian entrepreneurs seem to have a guilt complex about the idea of making money. Profit is not a dirty word; it's the reason you're in business. It's the way you provide for your family. "The worker deserves his wages" (1 Timothy 5:18). Of course, you can use your business and its profits to bless other people. You can give money or volunteer your time to missionaries, your church, and worthy causes. You can feed the hungry or house the homeless. You can give free products to people who need them. You can minister through your business and with your profits, but the business itself is not a ministry.

It's helpful to understand different types of income. Linear income results from trading hours for dollars—that's what you earn when you're employed or when you provide services on a freelance basis. You work, and you get paid for it. If you want more money, you have to work again. That's how my editing business works: I edit a book, and I get paid for it. To make more money, I need to edit another book. Passive or residual income results when you work once and get paid for it over and over. This is the premise behind multilevel marketing companies. It's also what you get when you create a product to sell, receive royalties, or make wise investments.

When you have a salaried job or regular hourly wages from an employer, your income is predictable. When you have your own business, your income is variable. Cash flow fluctuates, unless you have regular clients who keep you on retainer. Good money-management skills are a must.

How can you increase your income? An obvious choice is to work more hours, but you can only take that so far or it can lead to burnout. If you sell on eBay or use affiliate links, you can focus on higher-priced items. If your income is linear, you can add residual income by creating your own products. If you sell your own products, you can try to reduce the costs of production to increase your profit margin. Whether you're selling products or services, you can raise your prices if the market will bear it. You can leverage your expertise, learn new skills, and offer premium services. We'll talk more about pricing later in this chapter.

Tracking Your Time

You need to know where your money is coming from. Whether you are trading hours for dollars or creating products, whether you bill by the hour or by the project, it can be very helpful to track your work hours. As the activity for chapter 4, you kept a time log of all your activities for at least a week. With a work time log, you'll focus only on time you spend on business.

There are two ways to track your work time: by the day or by the project. I do both. I document my work time every day and assess my business productivity every week as part of my weekly review. This is part of my self-accountability. If I need to work twenty-five hours a week but my time log shows that I'm averaging twelve hours a week, I know I need to discipline myself to work more consistently.

Be sure you record the project as well as the time, whether it's a service you're providing for someone else or a product you're creating. Keeping track of the hours you're spending on each project will help you know where your income is coming from, assess the value of your time, and determine your most profitable activities so that you can focus on them. Keeping a work time log really clarified which business activities I needed to eliminate and which ones I needed to increase.

Keep in mind that not all of your work hours will be billable to a client. There are at least four different ways you can spend your work time.

- **Income-Generating Activity.** This includes performing a service like editing, babysitting, or mowing yards and creating and selling products. Some people place marketing in this category because although you don't get paid directly to market yourself, it's what brings in the customers and clients.

- **Business Operations.** This includes planning, setting goals, and meeting with your mastermind team (more on masterminds later in this chapter).

- **Clerical Tasks.** This includes keeping records, filing, and paying bills. These tasks can be time-consuming and are often good candidates for outsourcing.

- **Education.** Investing in yourself by developing your knowledge and skills is part of investing in your business. This includes going to conferences, listening to teleseminars and podcasts, and reading articles and books in your field and about business in general.

Selling

If you want to make money in business, you have to sell. This may seem obvious, but many people who are in business absolutely hate and fear selling. One of my students told me, "I have a distaste for business skills." Someone else said, "I don't like sales. I don't like to feel that I'm selling someone on something they don't want." Of course, no legitimate businessperson wants to sell people something they don't want. The crucial issue is this: Are you providing valuable solutions to real people with real problems? If you are, it is perfectly legitimate to sell. In fact, it could be argued that if you have a solution and you are not letting people who need it know about it, you are actually harming them by not selling to them.

Another reason that some people are hesitant to sell is that they're afraid of hype. They don't want to be seen as the stereotypical used-car salesman. Everyone hates hype. It's ironic for me to write about sales and marketing because I have always considered myself one of the most hype-resistant people on the planet. I absolutely hate to feel like somebody is trying to sell me something. However, in the past few years as I've learned more about business, I've found that I'm actually attracted to some sales letters or websites that I once would have regarded as over the top with hype. What makes the difference? I had an "aha" moment when I heard marketing expert Joe Polish say, "Hype used ethically is just enthusiasm for what you're selling." Notice he uses the word *ethically*. Of course, hype can also be used unethically.

Why do some people perceive a message as hype while others perceive the very same message as enthusiasm? Maybe the difference is in whether the subject of the pitch is interesting to them. If I read an enthusiastic sales letter for tickets to the Super Bowl or the World Series, it would sound like hype to me because I'm not interested in sports. But if I read an enthusiastic sales letter for a new book about writing or a powerful strategy for marketing my business effectively, that's attractive and compelling to me because I'm passionately interested in those things. In fact, even as sales resistant as I am, I don't feel like I'm being sold when the product is something I really want. That's the secret right there. If you're selling to the people who really want what you have, you're not going to come across as pushy.

> In the modern world of business, it is useless to be a creative, original thinker unless you can also *sell* what you create.
> DAVID OGILVY
> *Confessions of an Advertising Man*

For you to be effective at selling, your customers have to know you, like you, and trust you. You have to have credibility. But don't be afraid to be enthusiastic about what you're selling. If you're not all that excited about it, why should your prospective customer be excited?

Pricing

How do you set prices for the products and services you sell? Consider these questions: How much money do you need? How much time can you work? What is the value of your time and expertise? What are you worth? What is the usual range of rates in your industry?

What do similar products cost? What will the market bear?

When you are just starting a service-based business, you need to charge lower prices than veterans in the industry. One of my coaching clients said she was uncomfortable because "there are other people who know so much more than I do and offer more than I do." That is always going to be true, no matter how much you learn. Everyone knows different things and has a different level of expertise. You just need to have integrity. Be straightforward about what you can offer, but don't sell yourself short. Don't make promises you can't keep. Underpromise and overdeliver.

As your skills and experience increase and as demand for your service grows, raise your prices accordingly. I reached a point where more people were asking me to edit their books than I had time to serve. One of my regular clients told me, "You need to raise your rates—even for me." I've been editing since 1986, so my rates now run toward the higher end of the industry scale. Thankfully, my clients agree that my expertise is worth the price.

Never position yourself just on pricing, though, because somebody can always undercut your prices. There are other ways to distinguish yourself—for example, excellent quality, speed of service, or wonderful testimonials. I was disappointed when a prospective client told me that he had heard I was an affordable editor. That is not how I want to position myself because it doesn't reflect the value of what I'm offering. In addition, clients who are shopping strictly on the basis of price are often hard to work with.

Raising your rates can be scary. Yes, you probably will lose some business. But you may also gain some new customers who wouldn't have used you at your lower rate because your services seemed too cheap. That may sound odd, but price affects perception. The most expensive item or service isn't necessarily the best, but most people believe you get what you pay for.

A lot depends on your target market. Are you targeting a high-end market or the economy, low-budget market? Or are you somewhere in the middle? A busy corporate executive is willing and able to pay higher prices for my editing and coaching than a cash-strapped solopreneur who's just starting her own business. I don't charge them different rates for the same work; rather, I offer different levels of service at different prices.

As I mentioned earlier, you can leverage your expertise, learn new skills, and offer premium services for a premium price. You can also train other people to do what you do, which is what I do with my editing course. Yes, it may create competition, but it can also create a workforce to whom you can confidently subcontract or outsource work. You can also offer group coaching and one-on-one coaching. A few years ago I realized I could help authors much more if I worked with them *before* they had completed their manuscripts. Coaching first-time authors through the process of choosing a topic, organizing their material, writing the book, selecting from among publishing options, and marketing their book has been both fulfilling and profitable.

If you are still uncomfortable about setting prices, remember to focus on the value you offer. If you are designing websites, for example, how much time, effort, and money are you saving your clients by designing it for them instead of them neglecting their business to take time to learn HTML and do it themselves? If you're creating a business site, your work will help them make more money than they paid you. People are willing to pay for solutions to their problems.

Also consider the value of your time and what else you could be doing with your time. For example, if you can make the same amount of money in twenty hours instead of thirty just by raising your prices to reflect what you're worth, what else might you do with those extra ten hours? Could you spend more time with your family? Could you get more rest and exercise and take better care of your health? I'm not advocating taking advantage of your clients with shady business practices, but don't take advantage of yourself or your family by charging less than what you're worth.

Marketing

Another big challenge, especially when you are just getting started, is finding customers and clients. How do you find them? Marketing.

When I say marketing, the first thing that may spring to mind is advertising. In a media-saturated age, traditional advertising is losing some of its power and effectiveness. Many exposures to any ad are usually required for a consumer to take action, and advertising can be very expensive. Publicity is an excellent—and free—way to increase awareness of your business. For example, having a newspaper article written about you or writing an article for a magazine can be much more effective in reaching your audience than a paid advertisement in the same publication.

Getting repeat business from satisfied clients is easier than finding new clients. Your current customer is your most valuable customer because it's much harder and more expensive to win a brand-new customer. If somebody already knows you, likes you, and trusts you enough to buy from you, he will probably buy from you again. Do you want a deal—a single transaction—or do you want a business? What are you doing to keep your customers coming back? You should always ask yourself, "What's next? What's the next logical product or service I can offer my customers?"

A great way to gain new clients is through referrals from satisfied clients. For the first three years of editing full time as a single mom, about three-fourths of my business came from referrals from one client who was a one-woman word-of-mouth volunteer marketing machine. When a client thanks you for doing a great job, don't hesitate to ask, "Do you know anyone else who might be interested in my services?" Many people are glad to refer their friends to someone who has proven to be skilled and reliable. Ask satisfied clients for a testimonial as well. These are very powerful marketing tools because a testimonial is someone else validating what you're saying about yourself.

Another good way to find new clients is through networking. A lot of business is about relationships. It really is not just what you know; it's also who you know and who knows you. Networking can be kind of expensive because you have to be where the people are. For example, you might join a local club, attend a regional business event, or travel to a business conference or event specific to your industry.

During a break at one business conference I attended, I had a short conversation with one of the speakers and later did some editing for him. Although he ultimately chose not to complete that project, his business partner saw enough of my work to know that he liked what I was doing. A year later, the partner saw me at another conference and asked me to help him with his own book. That became my most profitable editing project up until that point and helped me develop my "Tell Me Your Book" system, which ultimately led to multiple speaking opportunities. All of that developed because of one conversation with one speaker at one conference. That's the power of networking.

An important part of marketing has to do with perspective. Are you thinking from your perspective (what you want to sell) or from your customers' perspective (what they want to buy)? You must always answer this question for the customer: "What's in it for me?" This is such an important question that it has its own acronym— WIIFM (pronounced *wiff-em*). What benefit will the customer gain by buying from you? What problem will your product or service solve?

One of the transforming moments in my business was a conversation with marketing expert Martin Wales at a conference. The first time I met him, I was a little taken aback because he critiqued my business card. This then became a running joke. For several years, every time I saw him, he evaluated my latest business card. That's a valuable service coming from someone like Martin. What he told me in our first conversation has always stuck with me:

"When you're meeting someone at an event like this and he says, 'Hi, I'm Fred. I do so and so. What do you do?' he doesn't really want to know what you do. What he's asking is, 'What can you do for me?'"

When you're promoting your business, remember, it's not about your business; it's about what your business can do for the customer. Don't talk about your business and all its bells and whistles. Talk about the benefits that those features will provide to your customers.

Thinking from the customer's perspective is a huge part of copywriting. Copywriting is an incredibly valuable skill no matter what business you're in. It's been described as salesmanship in print and as a conversation with the customer. You need to speak the customer's language. How does the prospective customer think about his problem? What language does he use to describe it? Write this down and hang it in your office as a reminder:

Customers want to know, "What's in it for me?"

Working with Customers and Clients

Once you have customers and clients, what should you do with them? Always make sure to deliver what you've promised, and do your best to exceed their expectations.

However, providing excellent service does not mean making yourself personally available 24/7. Even though clients and customers are essential to your business, they can also be interruptions that keep you from getting your work done. You have to train them about how to work with you. If you don't want to accept incoming phone calls from prospects, don't post your phone number on your website; post your e-mail address instead. If you want or need to accept calls, post specific hours and let voice mail or an answering service pick up at other times. If you need to provide customer service or tech support for a product, answer as many questions as you can with a Frequently Asked Questions (FAQ) section on your website. You can also cut and paste from this FAQ to reply to e-mail inquiries. Better yet, hire a virtual assistant to handle routine inquiries.

One of my students told me, "I never get to have dinner with my family because customers always call at dinner time." That's just not worth the sacrifice, in my opinion. I urged her to consider other options, but she was reluctant because she wanted to put a personal touch in her business. The personal touch is a wonderful bonus when you can provide it, but there's always a trade-off. If you spend a lot of time with one customer, you may be losing other potential business by giving up time you could be spending on other, more profitable activities. As always, you have to find the right balance. If you need to be available for customer support, schedule specific phone hours and set up an online support system as well.

While making decisions about when and how to communicate with prospects, customers, and current clients, you have to ask yourself what you want your life to be like and how your business needs to operate to allow that. You are responsible for establishing boundaries and setting expectations. How well this works will depend partly on the demand for what you offer and how much people want to work with you. Marketing guru Dan Kennedy refuses to accept phone calls or e-mails; he accepts faxes only. That sounds odd, but it works for him because he has successfully positioned himself as a valuable (and high-priced) consultant. Prospective clients who really want to work with him are willing to jump through his hoops.

This may sound like a risky strategy. Won't you lose some prospective customers or clients if you're not available when they want to talk with you? Perhaps, but remember that you can't please everybody all the time. Do you really want to work with super-demanding clients? Maybe you do, if the price is right. Or maybe no fee would persuade you to throw your entire family's life into upheaval just to keep the client happy. Only you can make that decision.

Sometimes you just need to follow your gut instinct that a prospective client isn't worth it. I once met an aspiring author who wanted me to work on a book for him. He didn't have a complete manuscript, so he cut and pasted bits and pieces of text into twenty-five different e-mails. He then expected me to give him a price quote based on the word count. He repeated questions that I had already answered multiple times. Finally, he asked for my home phone number and a list of available times when he could call me. I wrote back with a list of three times when I could provide him with a fifteen-minute consultation and asked him to e-mail me his list of questions to make our time more effective. I never heard from him again, and frankly I was relieved. Even though I had space in my schedule for another client, he would have been way more trouble than his business was worth. On the other hand, a current editing client was impressed when I offered two different time options for calling her to discuss her book. As a corporate executive, she understood the value of my time as well as hers.

> It is also a good plan every now and then to go away and have a little relaxation; for then when you come back to the work your judgment will be surer, since to remain constantly at work will cause you to lose the power of judgment.
> LEONARDO DA VINCI
> *Leonardo da Vinci's Note-books* (trans. Edward McCurdy)

Mastermind Team

One of the most useful things I've done to build my business is to be part of a mastermind team. A mastermind team is a group of like-minded people from noncompeting businesses with similar goals who meet regularly to brainstorm, share goals, provide accountability, and encourage one another. The best teams include a variety of people who bring different strengths, talents, and weaknesses to the table so that they complement one another. Four to five people make a good-sized group.

My first mastermind group developed out of an all-night conversation on the last night of a business conference. I didn't get back to my room until 5:30 a.m., but it was worth it because I developed some very deep and lasting friendships. We met weekly by phone for about a year and a half, and we still stay in touch.

We limited our weekly phone call to ninety minutes and took turns being the moderator. We opened with prayer, and then each person quickly shared a success she wanted to celebrate, a challenge she had met, or an obstacle she had overcome. Then we allotted ten to fifteen minutes to brainstorm solutions to each person's biggest current challenge, and we closed with prayer. We also kept in touch and shared our goals by e-mail throughout the course of the week.

My second mastermind team had four members, all of whom I also met at a business conference.

> Two are better than one because they have a good return for their labor. For if either of them falls, the one will lift up his companion. But woe to the one who falls when there is not another to lift him up. Furthermore, if two lie down together they keep warm, but how can one be warm alone? And if one can overpower him who is alone, two can resist him. A cord of three strands is not quickly torn apart.
> ECCLESIASTES 4:9–12

After that I worked with an individual accountability partner for a while, and I'm currently on my third mastermind team—a dynamic group of four women with different businesses in the publishing industry. We talk on the phone only occasionally. Instead, we keep in touch using a private Facebook group where we share prayer requests and business challenges, help one another brainstorm solutions, and celebrate one another's successes. We also get together in person for an annual retreat. I had met only one of my three current teammates in person before starting the group, but we all knew one another very well online. I met two of these dear friends in person for the first time after we had already been a team for a year.

Being an entrepreneur can be lonely. A mastermind team can add accountability, a fresh perspective, a listening ear, wise counsel, and encouragement, thus strengthening both you and your business.

Record Keeping and Finances

Now I want to address a few practical things about working from home. This part has to come with a disclaimer: I'm not an accountant, and I'm not a lawyer. This is not legal advice. It's not tax advice, and it's not accounting advice. I'm just passing along a few of the tips I've picked up along the way for handling the record-keeping aspect of a home business.

Be sure to check state and local regulations for running a home business and obtain any required licenses and permits. You'll also need to learn about collecting and paying sales tax if you sell products or even some services. You can find out more online at the U.S. Small Business Administration.[1]

The IRS website called "The Small Business and Self-Employed Tax Center" provides a lot of information about self-employment, independent contracting, using an Employer Identification Number (EIN), deductible business expenses, depreciation, small business forms and publications, federal and state agencies, and so on.[2]

When you are self-employed as a sole proprietor, you don't get a

W-2 form like an employee to attach to your Form 1040. Instead, you fill out a "Schedule C: Profit or Loss from Business" to account for your business expenses and income. You may have to pay taxes once a quarter instead of once a year, and you'll have to pay self-employment tax as well as federal income tax. These are things an accountant can help you with. I hire an accountant to do my taxes; that is definitely something I want to outsource. Be sure to keep careful records of your income and expenses along with documentation. I keep copies of invoices, check stubs or photocopies of checks, receipts for expenses, and so on.

> Most small businesses fail because of poor accounting. . . . Proverbs 27:23 says, "Be diligent to know the state of your flocks and herds."
> DAVE RAMSEY
> *Entreleadership*

Be sure to open a separate checking account for your business. This may seem obvious, but when I started out, I didn't do that. I was in such a financial crisis that I poured all the income right into my living expenses, but that's not the way to do it. Maintaining a separate checking account for business keeps things clean for the IRS and helps you keep better records.

For more information about the financial and legal aspects of running a business, explore the resources in the notes and appendix A. You may also wish to consult an accountant and/or an attorney.

Include Your Children in Your Business

In chapter 7 we talked about the importance of balancing accessibility with boundaries for your children. We focused primarily on boundaries there. Now let's take another look at accessibility.

When you're working at home, it's easy to think, "I know I'm busy, but at least I'm here." But I know very well from experience that I'm not always "here." Try to be really *there* in your heart and in your head during family time so that you're not always keeping one foot in your home office and thinking, "I just need to write a couple more pages and ship a couple more boxes."

A single mom I coached put it this way: "I don't want my children to remember me as the mom who worked all the time. I value them above my business, and I want to walk that out." Once again, you have to find the right balance. You are working *for* your children— to provide for their physical needs—but you have to be sure to provide for their emotional and spiritual needs as well. You must make it very clear that although your work is important, you value them more.

We've looked at lots of strategies for balancing all our commitments. Here's one more: Involve your children in your business. This isn't always possible, but when it is, it can be very helpful and even fruitful. For example, many companies that publish homeschool curriculum are family-wide enterprises. You've probably encountered helpful homeschool students at conferences answering questions about their products, taking orders, and operating the cash register.

Here are just a few ways children can contribute to their family's business: designing and maintaining websites, graphic design, customer service, packing and shipping orders, taking inventory, selecting books to sell, baking, farming, sewing, cleaning, electrical contracting, lawn care, and maintaining rental properties.

Including your children in your business helps build their interest in your work so that they don't resent it, and it makes them feel like they're part of the family enterprise. The work teaches them responsibility and trains them in practical skills they can use to provide for their own future families.

Take Action!

☐ Would a home-based business be a good fit for your family? If this interests you, be sure to discuss it with your husband (if you're married) and pray for God's guidance.

☐ What kind of home business would work best for you? Do you want to work for a company as a home-based employee or independent contractor, or would you prefer to start your own business? How can you balance your passion with what the market is looking for?

☐ If you have a home business, what can you outsource so that you can focus on what you do best and what brings the most value for your time?

☐ Do you dislike selling? What can you do to become more skilled and comfortable with sales?

☐ How will you market your products/services to find customers/clients? What's in it for them?

☐ Do you have a mastermind team? If not, identify several like-minded people and suggest forming a team.

☐ Are you comfortable and responsible with the record-keeping and financial aspects of running a business? Be sure to seek the help you may need from an accountant and/or an attorney.

☐ How can you include your children in your business?

CHAPTER 16

Moving Ahead

I have learned that success is to be measured not so much by the position that one has reached in life as by the obstacles which he has overcome while trying to succeed.
BOOKER T. WASHINGTON
Up From Slavery

Tools and strategies are only as good as the action you take on them. Perhaps you get comfortable and start to slack off. Other times, things may go wrong despite your best efforts. Perfection isn't possible; steady progress is the goal. When things fall apart, pick yourself up, dust yourself off, and get back to working your plan. You may need to adjust your goals and try some new strategies. Remember, do what works for you and your family.

How Do You Know When It's Not Working?

Some of my students ask, "How do you know when it's not working? What's the signal that things are not going as planned?" Sometimes it's pretty obvious when things aren't working, but staying alert to the early signs of trouble can help you avoid crashing and burning. Here are a few of the warning signs.

When you do your assessment at the end of each week, you keep writing "No." Lots of your goals are not met—you didn't do this one, didn't do that one, didn't do the other one. That's going to happen sometimes, but if week after week you find yourself consistently writing "no" next to your goals, either you're setting unrealistic goals or something unexpected is keeping you from meeting realistic goals.

Things keep slipping through the cracks. We've all experienced this. Missing deadlines, paying bills late, not returning phone calls, and forgetting appointments may happen occasionally. But if such incidents are frequent, it's a signal that your life is out of balance.

Things are messy and cluttered. A cluttered desk is a big clue. A cluttered purse is always a sign that I need to take time to sort and file receipts, clear out the kids' gum wrappers, and so on. A cluttered car is another clue. When the front passenger seat of my van is piled high with stuff, I know I'm becoming disorganized and I haven't been taking care of things as they happen. A messy house is a sign that life is out of balance. Now

> Each of us needs to seek his or her own level of involvement and not let the standard be mandated by the often exorbitant expectations of others. . . . We must understand that everyone has a different tolerance for overload and a different threshold level when breakdown begins to occur. It is important for us to set people free to seek their own level.
> Richard A. Swenson, MD
> *Margin*

you may be thinking this is life as usual, and I assure you that my home has its share of routine clutter. I'm talking about an unusual amount of it—a burdensome level where all you see is the mess.

Your relationships are suffering. When your life is out of balance, your relationships suffer. If you're feeling out of touch with God, maybe you're not spending enough time in prayer, studying the Bible, and fellowshipping with other believers. If your relationships with your family are suffering, it may be because you've been short-tempered or you're shortchanging them. ("I'm sorry, but we can't play a game tonight like we planned because I just have too much to do.") I speak from experience here—I have been guilty of this many times.

You spend a lot of time just puttering around. You randomly spend your time on low-priority things instead of taking care of the important ones because you feel so overwhelmed by your to-do list. This is often a signal that you need some targeted time to rest instead of just half pretending to work, half not really doing anything. That doesn't get anything accomplished, nor does it give you the physical or emotional rest you need.

You're frequently irritable, exhausted, frustrated, and overwhelmed. We all feel this way now and then, but if it becomes typical, your life is definitely out of balance and you need to make some changes.

What Do You Do When It's Not Working?

Seek God's guidance. The first thing, of course, is to pray for God's direction in your life. A dear friend went through a season when most of the things in her life, except for her family relationships, seemed to be collapsing. She and her husband spent a lot of time in prayer trying to discern what God was trying to teach them through this.

Examine yourself. Are you simply trying to do too much? Are you taking on burdens that aren't yours to bear? Do you need to eliminate some responsibilities and say no to everything but the essentials for a while? Start focusing on what's most important, and don't be afraid to ask for help.

Seek wise counsel. Even when you're being honest with yourself, getting another perspective can prove invaluable. Seek godly counsel from your spouse, pastor, friend, mastermind team, or coach, and see what you may need to change. Somebody outside can often see things that we're blind to in our own lives. One time I was coaching a client about finding balance in her life, and at the end of that conversation, I realized that some of the things I had said to her were things I needed somebody to say to me.

> It is not by irregular efforts, however gigantic, that any great practical achievement is overtaken. It is by the constant recurrence and repetition of small efforts directed to a given object, and resolutely sustained and persevered in.
> THOMAS CHALMERS
> Scottish minister

Use the tools. In this book we've explored dozens of strategies for finding balance in your life. If your problem is that you are overwhelmed and not getting everything done, repeating the time log exercise can be useful. If you feel as if you're wandering and don't know what you need to do next, you might want to look again at your Big Dream, your goals, and your priorities, then make sure your Weekly Plan and Daily Tasks reflect those and eliminate what doesn't. If you're simply exhausted, put on your oxygen mask by doing something creative or relaxing.

Be Decisive

Once you have evaluated your situation and learned how to use the various strategies and tools in this book, you have to take action in order to move forward. Don't flounder in indecision or second-guess yourself. Pick something to try and do it. If it doesn't work, try something else. Be decisive. Decisiveness is one of the traits common to most successful people.

F. Scott Fitzgerald's notes for his fifth novel, *The Love of the Last Tycoon*, include an interesting story that dramatically illustrates the quality of decisiveness. MGM producer Irving Thalberg, who was regarded as the boy wonder of the movie industry, was Fitzgerald's model for his hero, Monroe Stahr. In a conversation with Fitzgerald, Thalberg discussed a scenario in which a road must be cut through a mountain and there are half a dozen equally good possible locations for the road. He said:

> Great things are not done by impulse, but by a series of small things brought together.
> VINCENT VAN GOGH

"Now suppose you happen to be the top man, there's a point where you don't exercise the faculty of judgment in the ordinary way, but simply the faculty of arbitrary decision. You say, 'Well, I think we will put the road there' and you trace it with your finger and you know in your secret heart and no one else knows, that you have no reason for putting the road there rather than in several other different courses, but you're the only person that knows that you don't know why you're doing it and you've got to stick to that and you've got to pretend that you know and that you did it for specific reasons even though you're utterly assailed by doubt at times as to the wisdom of your decision because all these other possible decisions keep echoing in your ear."[1]

Remember, there's seldom one right way to do something. There's a point at which you cannot continue to gather information—you must make a decision. Once you've made the decision, move ahead and don't keep second-guessing yourself. Don't be afraid to admit when you're wrong, but don't agonize over those other possible decisions that keep echoing in your ear. Make a decision, move ahead, and then learn from your mistakes and do it better next time.

Don't Wait for the Most Favorable Conditions

The final thought I want to leave you with comes from C. S. Lewis, who was commenting about how people could justify focusing on education when a war was going on:

> If we let ourselves, we shall always be waiting for some distraction or other to end before we can really get down to our work. The only people who achieve much are those who want knowledge so badly that they seek it while the conditions are still unfavorable. Favorable conditions never come.[2]

I urge you not to wait until the conditions are favorable or perfect to follow your dreams. There's never an ideal time. Start where you are, with what you have, and with what you know now. Then continue to learn, grow, and reach higher while taking care of your family, your business, and yourself.

Take Action!

❏ Complete the Post-Book Progress Check in appendix B to measure your progress and identify those areas you still need to work on.

❏ Be decisive. Make a commitment to take action on what you've learned in this book. Don't try to do it all at once. Instead, focus on building one new habit or trying one new strategy at a time.

❏ Stay alert to early signs of trouble to avoid burnout. If you're feeling overwhelmed or discouraged, remember to find peace in the space between the ideal and reality. Above all, seek God's guidance and rest in His faithfulness.

Recommended Resources

I have read and learned from every book recommended here. Many other excellent resources are available in each of these categories, but I have limited the list to those that have been meaningful and helpful to me personally. Many of them have had a profound influence on my life, especially in my early years of motherhood and homeschooling. I pray they will be a blessing to you as well.

LIFE MANAGEMENT
Getting Things Done: The Art of Stress-Free Productivity by David Allen

Discipline: The Glad Surrender by Elisabeth Elliot

Freedom from Tyranny of the Urgent by Charles E. Hummel

Tyranny of the Urgent by Charles E. Hummel

Ordering Your Private World by Gordon MacDonald

Redeeming the Time: A Christian Approach to Work and Leisure by Leland Ryken

In Search of Balance: Keys to a Stable Life by Richard A. Swenson

Margin: Restoring Emotional, Physical, Financial, and Time Reserves to Overloaded Lives by Richard A. Swenson

The Overload Syndrome: Learning to Live within Your Limits by Richard A. Swenson

Cozi (www.cozi.com)—an app for sharing calendars, to-do lists, shopping lists, and more with your family

Evernote (www.evernote.com)—an app for accessing all your notes, web clips, files, and images on every device and computer you use

FAMILY LIFE
The Shaping of a Christian Family: How My Parents Nurtured My Faith by Elisabeth Elliot

For the Family's Sake: The Value of Home in Everyone's Life by Susan Schaeffer Macaulay

Desperate: Hope for the Mom Who Needs to Breathe by Sarah Mae and Sally Clarkson

What Is a Family? by Edith Schaeffer

Hints on Child Training by H. Clay Trumbull

7 Tools for Cultivating Your Child's Potential by Zan Tyler

Full-Time Parenting: A Guide to Family-Based Discipleship by Israel Wayne

HOMEMAKING

Clutter's Last Stand: It's Time To De-junk Your Life! by Don Aslett

Is There Life After Housework? A Revolutionary Approach to Cutting Your Cleaning Time 75% by Don Aslett

401 Ways to Get Your Kids to Work at Home by Bonnie Runyan McCullough and Susan Walker Monson

The Busy Mom's Guide to a Happy, Organized Home: Fast Solutions to Hundreds of Everyday Dilemmas by Kathy Peel

The Hidden Art of Homemaking: Creative Ideas for Enriching Everyday Life by Edith Schaeffer

EDUCATION

A Charlotte Mason Companion: Personal Reflections on the Gentle Art of Learning by Karen Andreola

The Three R's by Ruth Beechick (grades K–3)

You Can Teach Your Child Successfully by Ruth Beechick (grades 4-8)

The Ultimate Guide to Homeschooling by Debra Bell

Teaching the Trivium: Christian Homeschooling in a Classical Style by Harvey and Laurie Bluedorn

The Homeschool Journey: Windows into the Heart of a Learning Family by Susan and Michael Card

Educating the WholeHearted Child by Clay and Sally Clarkson

101 Top Picks for Homeschool Curriculum: Choosing the Right Curriculum and Approach for Each Child's Learning Style by Cathy Duffy

Weapons of Mass Instruction: A Schoolteacher's Journey Through the Dark World of Compulsory Schooling by John Taylor Gatto

Endangered Minds: Why Children Don't Think—and What We Can Do About It by Jane Healy

Failure to Connect: How Computers Affect Our Children's Minds—and What We Can Do About It by Jane Healy

For the Children's Sake: Foundations of Education for Home and School by Susan Schaeffer Macaulay

Homeschooling Methods: Seasoned Advice on Learning Styles, edited by Paul & Gena Suarez

Home Ed Expert (www.HomeEdExpert.com)—an online system to help you find curricula and resources that fit your goals and teaching style as well as your students' unique needs and learning styles

Home School Legal Defense Association (www.HSLDA. org)

READING

How to Read a Book: The Classic Guide to Intelligent Reading by Mortimer J. Adler and Charles Van Doren

Who Should We Then Read? volumes 1 and 2 by Jan Bloom

Read for the Heart: Whole Books for WholeHearted Families by Sarah Clarkson

Shelf Life: How Books Have Changed the Destinies and Desires of Men and Nations by George Grant and Karen Grant

Honey for a Child's Heart: The Imaginative Use of Books in Family Life by Gladys Hunt

How to Grow a Young Reader: Books from Every Age for Readers of Every Age by Kathryn Lindskoog and Ranelda Mack Hunsicker

Eclectic Bibliophile (www.eclecticbibliophile.com)—my blog for book lovers

SINGLE PARENTS
My Single Mom Life: True Stories and Practical Lessons for Your Journey by Angela Thomas

"Single {Not Alone}" by Michael Donnelly, The Home School Court Report (January/February 2011), www.hslda.org/courtreport/V27N1/V27N101.asp

"Single-Parent Homeschooling" by Mary Jo Tate, "Home School Heartbeat" radio show, vol. 93, programs 1–5, October 19–23, 2009, www.hslda.org/docs/hshb/93/hshbwk1.asp

"Single-Parent Homeschooling: How You Can Make It Work!" by Mary Jo Tate, recorded webinar through HSLDA, http://store.hslda.org/tate-mary-jo-c237.aspx

The Book Samaritan (www.thebooksamaritan.com)—provides homeschool materials to families in need

Home School Foundation (www.homeschoolfoundation.org)—assists homeschooling families in need

Single Parents at Home (www.singleparentsathome.com)—my blog for single parents

HOME BUSINESS
Free Marketing: 101 Low and No-Cost Ways to Grow Your Business Online and Off by Jim Cockrum

Good to Great: Why Some Companies Make the Leap . . . and Others Don't by Jim Collins

Home-Based Business for Dummies by Paul Edwards, Sarah Edwards, and Peter Economy

Tribes: We Need You to Lead Us by Seth Godin

Platform: Get Noticed in a Noisy World by Michael Hyatt

EntreLeadership: 20 Years of Practical Business Wisdom from the Trenches by Dave Ramsey

Business Tips and Taxes for Writers by Carol Topp

APPENDIX B

Planning Forms

You can download customizable versions of these forms at
www.FlourishAtHome.com/book.

Pre-Book Self-Evaluation

1. What is the most frustrating aspect of your daily life?

2. What brings you the greatest satisfaction?

3. What are your biggest personal challenges?

4. What are your biggest family challenges?

5. What are your biggest business challenges?

6. What is currently missing in your life that you'd like to make time for?

7. Do you have written goals? Long-term and short-term?

8. If you could change just one thing about your life, what would it be?

Time Log

TIME	Sunday	Monday	Tuesday	Wednesday
12:00 AM				
12:30 AM				
1:00 AM				
1:30 AM				
2:00 AM				
2:30 AM				
3:00 AM				
3:30 AM				
4:00 AM				
4:30 AM				
5:00 AM				
5:30 AM				
6:00 AM				
6:30 AM				
7:00 AM				
7:30 AM				

Time Log

TIME	Sunday	Monday	Tuesday	Wednesday
8:00 AM				
8:30 AM				
9:00 AM				
9:30 AM				
10:00 AM				
10:30 AM				
11:00 AM				
11:30 AM				
12:00 PM				
12:30 PM				
1:00 PM				
1:30 PM				
2:00 PM				
2:30 PM				
3:00 PM				
3:30 PM				

TIME LOG

TIME	Sunday	Monday	Tuesday	Wednesday
4:00 PM				
4:30 PM				
5:00 PM				
5:30 PM				
6:00 PM				
6:30 PM				
7:00 PM				
7:30 PM				
8:00 PM				
8:30 PM				
9:00 PM				
9:30 PM				
10:00 PM				
10:30 PM				
11:00 PM				
11:30 PM				

TIME LOG

TIME	Thursday	Friday	Saturday
12:00 AM			
12:30 AM			
1:00 AM			
1:30 AM			
2:00 AM			
2:30 AM			
3:00 AM			
3:30 AM			
4:00 AM			
4:30 AM			
5:00 AM			
5:30 AM			
6:00 AM			
6:30 AM			
7:00 AM			
7:30 AM			

TIME LOG

TIME	Thursday	Friday	Saturday
8:00 AM			
8:30 AM			
9:00 AM			
9:30 AM			
10:00 AM			
10:30 AM			
11:00 AM			
11:30 AM			
12:00 PM			
12:30 PM			
1:00 PM			
1:30 PM			
2:00 PM			
2:30 PM			
3:00 PM			
3:30 PM			

TIME LOG

TIME	Thursday	Friday	Saturday
4:00 PM			
4:30 PM			
5:00 PM			
5:30 PM			
6:00 PM			
6:30 PM			
7:00 PM			
7:30 PM			
8:00 PM			
8:30 PM			
9:00 PM			
9:30 PM			
10:00 PM			
10:30 PM			
11:00 PM			
11:30 PM			

BIG DREAM

1. What would I be doing if nothing stood in my way?

2. What stands in my way?

3. What do I need to do to achieve my goals?

YEARLY REVIEW

PERSONAL

FAMILY

BUSINESS

SERVICE

READING

YEARLY GOALS

What you can do, or dream you can, begin it. Boldness has genius, power, and magic in it.
JOHN ANSTER's translation of Goethe's *Faust*

PERSONAL

FAMILY

BUSINESS

SERVICE

READING

Monthly Calendar

Month of _____

Sunday	Monday	Tuesday	Wednesday	Thursday	Friday	Saturday

WEEKLY PLAN

Look at a day when you are supremely satisfied at the end. It's not a day when you lounge around doing nothing; it's when you've had everything to do, and you've done it.

MARGARET THATCHER

Week of _____

PERSONAL

FAMILY

BUSINESS

SERVICE

READING

Post-Book Progress Check

Before responding to this Post-Book Progress Check, take a few minutes to review your answers to the Pre-Book Self-Evaluation to help you gauge your progress.

1. What have you learned to help you deal with the most frustrating aspect of your daily life? What difference has it made?

2. What have you learned that allows you to experience more of what brings you the greatest satisfaction? What difference has it made?

3. What have you learned that has helped with your biggest personal challenges? What difference has it made?

4. What have you learned that has helped you with your biggest family challenges? What difference has it made?

5. What have you learned that has helped you with your biggest business challenges? What difference has it made?

6. What have you learned that will help you make time for whatever has been missing in your life? What difference has it made?

7. If you didn't have written goals before, do you have them now? How has this helped? If you already had written goals, how have you changed your approach to setting goals?

8. Have you found a way to change the one thing about your life that you'd like to change? (Note: This one may take a bit more time than the others to see results.)

9. What is your biggest remaining challenge? How will you take action to work on it?

NOTES

CHAPTER 3

1. Elisabeth Elliot, *Shadow of the Almighty* (Peabody, MA: Hendrickson, 2008), 112–113.

2. Elisabeth Elliot, *A Lamp Unto My Feet: The Bible's Light for Your Daily Walk* (Ventura, CA: Regal, 2004), Day 14.

3. Brady Boyd, *Sons and Daughters: Spiritual Orphans Finding Our Way Home* (Grand Rapids, MI: Zondervan, 2012), 117.

4. Marilyn Rockett, *Homeschooling at the Speed of Life* (Nashville: B&H Publishing Group, 2007), 19.

5. Stephanie Winston, *Getting Organized,* revised edition (New York: Grand Central Publishing, 2006), 12.

6. Eileen Roth, *Organizing for Dummies* (New York: Hungry Minds, Inc., 2001), 285.

CHAPTER 5

1. Essex Cholmondeley, *The Story of Charlotte Mason: 1842–1923* (Darlington, Durham, England: J. M. Dent, 1960), 160.

CHAPTER 6

1. Jan Karon, "Leaving Mitford: Jan Karon on Life and Writing," The Christian Broadcasting Network, http://www. cbn.com/entertainment/Books/elliott_JanKaron.aspx (accessed September 16, 2013).

2. Jim Collins, *Good to Great* (New York: Harper Collins, 2011), 11.

CHAPTER 7

1. C. S. Lewis, *The Collected Letters of C. S. Lewis, vol. 2: Books, Broadcasts, and the War, 1931–1949* (New York: Harper Collins, 2004), 595.

2. Maud Monahan, *The Life and Letters of Janet Erskine Stuart* (New York: Longmans Green, 1922), 93.

CHAPTER 8

1. Edith Schaeffer, *The Hidden Art of Homemaking* (Wheaton, IL: Tyndale House, 1971), 209.

CHAPTER 9
1. G. S. Reaney, *Mothers and Motherhood* (1896), as quoted in Clay and Sally Clarkson, *Educating the WholeHearted Child* (Anderson, IN: Apologia, 2011), 310.

2. Charles H. Spurgeon, *Morning and Evening* (Grand Rapids, MI: Zondervan, 1980), June 12 morning reading.

3. Brother Lawrence, *The Practice of the Presence of God with Spiritual Maxims* (Grand Rapids, MI: Spire Books, 1967), 12.

4. Winston Churchill, *The Gathering Storm*, vol. 1 of *The Second World War* (Boston: Houghton Mifflin Harcourt, 1985), 375.

CHAPTER 10
1. Barbara Bush, *Barbara Bush: A Memoir* (New York: Macmillan, 1995), 570.

CHAPTER 11
1. Gene Weingarten, "Pearls Before Breakfast," *The Washington Post* (April 8, 2007), http://www.washingtonpost.com/wp-dyn/content/article/2007/04/04/AR2007040401721.html.

CHAPTER 12
1. Brother Lawrence, *The Practice of the Presence of God*, 11.

2. Gigi Graham Tchividjian, "Meaning in the Mundane," *Christian Parenting Today* (January/February 1990), 72.

CHAPTER 13

1. Dr. Brian Ray and HSLDA, "Homeschool Progress Report 2009," HSLDA, http://store.nexternal.com/hslda/homeschool-progress-report-2009-p48.aspx (accessed September 16, 2013).

2. Mike Smith, "How Do Homeschoolers Fare in the Work place?" *Homeschool Heartbeat*, volume 59, program 16 (April 18, 2005).

3. Dr. Brian Ray and HSLDA, "Homeschooling Grows Up," HSLDA, http://store.nexternal.com/hslda/homeschooling-grows-up-p19.aspx (accessed September 16, 2013).

4. Home Ed Expert, www.HomeEdExpert.com (accessed September 16, 2013).

5. HSLDA, http://hslda.org/ (accessed September 16, 2013).

6. Eudora Welty, *One Writer's Beginnings* (Cambridge, MA: Harvard University Press, 1984), 5.

7. Karen Andreola, *A Charlotte Mason Companion* (Charlotte Mason Research & Supply, 1998), 41–42.

CHAPTER 15

1. Small Business Administration, "Obtain Licenses and Permits," http://www.sba.gov/licenses-and-permits (accessed September 16, 2013).

2. Internal Revenue Service, "Small Business and Self-Employed Tax Center," http://www.irs.gov/businesses/small/index.html (accessed September 16, 2013).

CHAPTER 16

1. F. Scott Fitzgerald, *The Love of the Last Tycoon: A Western*, ed. Matthew J. Bruccoli (Cambridge, England: Cambridge University Press, 2003), xviii.

2. C. S. Lewis, "Learning in War-Time," *The Weight of Glory* (New York: Harper Collins, 2009), 60.

Contact Mary Jo

Flourish **Bonuses, Updates, and Resources**

www.FlourishAtHome.com/book

SPEAKING

Mary Jo loves to speak to moms about how to balance their busy lives so they can flourish. Her most popular topics include:

- How Do You Do It All? Balancing Family Life and Home Business in the Real World

- Just Say No: Overcoming Interruptions and Distractions

- FREEDOM: A Toolbox of Practical Strategies to Help You Flourish at Home

- Single-Parent Homeschooling: How You Can Make It Work

- The Eclectic Bibliophile: Nurturing a Passion for Books and Building a Home Library

- Writing for Publication and Building a Writing Business

For details about these and other topics, or to contact Mary Jo about speaking at your event, visit: www.FlourishAtHome.com/speaking

LET'S CONNECT ONLINE

Blog: www.FlourishAtHome.com

Facebook: www.facebook.com/FlourishAtHome

Twitter: www.twitter.com/maryjotate

Pinterest: www.pinterest.com/flourishmom

Find Balance Faster with One-on-One Coaching!

As I've emphasized throughout this book, taking action on what you learn is essential if you really want to change your life. The action steps at the end of each chapter will help you get started, but my own experience has taught me that I get farther faster when I work with a coach.

If you would like personal help in applying the strategies you've learned in *Flourish* to your unique situation, I'd love to work with you one on one! My coaching includes:

- individual guidance
- powerful brainstorming
- customized problem solving
- ongoing accountability

I'll listen—*really listen*—to you and work with you to conquer your challenges and achieve your dreams. Sometimes I'll ask tough questions, and I'll do my best to stretch you and encourage you to grow, but always with compassion and understanding.

I can give this kind of personal attention to only a few people, so if you're ready to supercharge your progress, contact me today to apply for coaching!

www.flourishathome.com/coaching

"When it comes to clarity and focus, Mary Jo Tate has got it in spades. It must be the editor in her that gives her the ability to clear away the fluff and cut straight to the heart of the matter. Her well-formed questions and articulate coaching have saved me hours of deliberation and analysis. But I must warn you, don't even think about becoming accountable to her unless you're ready to get in motion and stay there. Her life is in momentum, and whatever she puts her hand to takes off running."
Louise Jones, Long Beach, California

"Mary Jo's giftedness as an accountability coach is unsurpassed. She somehow manages to see and speak the truth to me right when I need it most, but always in her own special 'firm but gentle' way. Unlike many self-proclaimed coaches, she genuinely walks her talk and leads by example. Mary Jo has personally developed tremendous self-discipline and time management systems to set and achieve entrepreneurial goals in life circumstances that have caused many to simply throw up their hands and throw in the towel. If you're tired of treating your dreams like a hobby, get serious and get coaching from Mary Jo!"
PATTI THOMPSON, Alcoa, Tennessee

"I love to be around people who make me think, who challenge me, and who have fresh new ideas to explore. Mary Jo Tate is one of those people. She always seems to come at a problem from angles that never occurred to me, and I learn from her each time we talk. She is both encouraging and challenging, and her advice has proved practical and helpful to me many times. If you want to get your ideas on a track to completion, I can think of no one who would be a better mentor than Mary Jo!"
MARILYN ROCKETT, Cypress, Texas

"Mary Jo Tate has coached me in areas where I have needed a push—sometimes a shove. Her time-management skills and positive get-it-done attitude have helped me to be much more effective with each minute. She has listened to my whole picture and then given me much-needed, honest criticism. Some of it was uncomfortable, but it's been exactly what I needed to move ahead. Our brainstorming sessions have yielded an abundance of well-put-together, practical ideas."
KATHERINE GOWAN, Louisville, Kentucky